Night & Day

Exploring the Divine Wisdom
in Duality

WAEL IBRAHIM
(Edited by Lyra.G)

BOOK TITLE CREDIT

My genius student:
RAHA ANWAR

Thank you.

Published by:

Unit No. E-10-5, Jalan SS 15/4G, Subang Square,
47500 Subang Jaya, Selangor, Malaysia
+603-5612-2407 (office) / +6017-399-7411 (mobile)
info@tertib.press
www.tertib.press
@tertibpress (Facebook & Instagram)

Author	:	Wael Ibrahim
Editor	:	Lyra. G
		Arisha Mohd Affendy
Proofreader	:	Ilyana Elisa
Cover designer	:	Abdul Adzim Md Daim
Typesetter	:	Abdul Adzim Md Daim

NIGHT & DAY: EXPLORING THE DIVINE WISDOM IN DUALITY

First Edition: December 2024

Perpustakaan Negara Malaysia

Cataloguing-in-Publication Data

A catalogue record for this book is available from the National Library of Malaysia

ISBN: 978-967-2844-38-9

Copyright © Wael Ibrahim 2024

All rights reserved.

No part of this publication may be reproduced, distributed, or transmitted in any form or by any means, including photocopying, recording, or other electronic or mechanical methods, without the prior written permission of Tertib Publishing.
Printed in Malaysia.

Contents

Dedication	1
Preface	3
Introduction	5
Light and Darkness	8
Light as Divine Illumination	9
The Prophet's Radiant Guidance: A Beacon in Darkness	10
Light as a Symbol of Guidance: Qur'anic Evidences	11
Darkness: The result of Ignorance and Evil	12
The Battle of *Badr*: A Manifestation of Light and Darkness	13
Light and Darkness in Rituals: *Ṣalah and Ramadan*	14
Conclusion Striving towards the Light	15
Life and Death	18
Life: A Divine Gift-Test and an Opportunity:	19
Death: A Transition to the Afterlife	21
The Soul: A Divine Trust	24
The Eternal Significance	26
Mercy and Wrath	29
Allah: The Most Merciful	30
The Concept of Allah's Wrath	32
The Mercy of Allah in Daily Life	33
Balancing Hope and Fear	35
The Harmonious Dichotomy	36

Creation and Destruction — 39
- Allah SWT: The Supreme Creator — 40
- Creation and Divine Wisdom — 41
- Destruction as a Consequence — 43
- Seeking Protection and Refuge — 45
- Submission to The Divine Will of Allah SWT — 46

Guidance and Misguidance — 49
- Allah: The Ultimate Guide — 50
- Human Responsibility and Free Will — 52
- The Qur'an as a Clear Guidance — 54
- Seeking Guidance through Prayer — 56
- The Struggle Against Misguidance — 58
- Navigating the Path of Guidance — 60

Jannah and *Jahannam* — 62
- Paradise (*Jannah*): The Unimaginable Eternal Bliss — 63
- Hell (*Jahannam*): The Awful Destination — 65
- Seeking Redemption through the Mercy of Allah SWT — 67
- The Eternal Symphony of Existence — 69

Knowledge and Ignorance — 71
- Knowledge as Divine Illumination — 72
- Ignorance: The Veil that Shrouds Understanding — 74
- The Balance: Seeking Knowledge with Humility — 76
- The Radiance of Enlightenment — 77

Forgiveness and Retribution — 80
- Allah's Oft-Forgiving Nature — 81
- Retribution: Consequences of Wrongdoing — 83
- The Intersection: Forgiveness and Retribution in Harmony — 85
- The Divine Justice and Mercy — 87

Prophets and their Opponents — 89
- The Divine Commission of Prophets — 90
- The Challenge of Opposition — 92
- The Divine Support for Prophets: — 94
- Navigating the Struggle: Lessons for Believers — 95
- Navigating the Path Amidst Opposition — 97

Free Will and Predestination — 99
- Free Will: The Gift of Choice — 100
- Predestination: The Divine Choice — 103
- The Harmonious Relationship: Understanding the Paradox — 105
- Embracing the *Qadr* of Allah SWT — 108

Angels and Satan — 111
- Angels: Agents of Divine Obedience — 112
- Satan (*Iblis*): The Defiant Deceiver — 114
- Lessons for Believers — 116
- Navigating the unseen — 117

Negatives and Positives: Navigating Ethical Dimensions in Islam — 120
- Negatives: Straying from Ethical Pathways — 121
- Positives: Embracing Virtues in Islam — 124
- Navigating Ethical Dimensions: Lessons for Believers — 126
- Ethical Excellence in Islam — 128

Final Thoughts — 130

To the incredible Faith Events and Tertib Publishing Teams:

Your dedication, kindness, and continuous support have been the driving force that helped bring out the best in me. This book is a witness to your tireless efforts and belief in my work.

Jazākhāllah khayran.

Working with you all has been a dream—though sometimes I wonder if you ever sleep.

Perhaps you're like books too: always awake because you're filled with too many weird and wonderful characters!

Love you all for the sake of Allah

Thank you for everything.

This book is as much yours as it is mine.

Wael Ibrahim

"...When we contemplate the universe, we see that Allah SWT has created for everything a natural adversary or an enemy. He created cotton and the worm that thrives upon it. He fashioned plants, and the locusts that devour them. He bestowed fruits upon us, alongside fungus that resides within them. He designed our nostrils, yet also created the flu that afflicts them. He formed our teeth, and the cavities that affect them."

Dr. Mostafa Mahmoud

Preface

In the name of Allah, the Most Merciful, the Most Compassionate, I welcome you all to "Night and Day: Exploring the Wisdom of Duality." Within the pages of this book, we embark on a profound journey guided by the light of the beautiful Qur'anic revelation and the teachings of our beloved Prophet Muhammad SAW.

Growing up in this very strange world, I have always found myself intrigued by what I call dualities of life—light and darkness, good and evil, joy and sorrow etc. These opposing forces have captivated my mind for many, many years. Before committing myself to the *deen*, and even after that. Such concepts and beauty that are not mere accidents but purposely and intentionally created by Allah SWT, the Most Exquisite and Magnificent so that we may ponder and acknowledge Him as the Ultimate Creator of all.

In "Night & Day," together we delve deep into the essence of divine pairs, recognising them as the defining elements of our existence that can never be altered or modified by any created being. For instance, every soul grapples with the eternal struggle between virtue and vice, and it is through the guidance of the Qur'an and the sunnah of our beloved Prophet SAW that we navigate this journey with wisdom and proper knowledge.

Through careful exploration and analysis, we uncover the profound wisdom concealed within these dualities that Allah SWT made very visible to every created being, enriching our understanding of the purpose and meaning of our existence. Concepts like compassion and retribution, life and death, creation and destruction are illuminated through the divine teachings of Allah SWT and His prophet SAW, offering invaluable perspectives that shape our perception of reality.

This book is an invitation for seekers of knowledge—those eager to delve deeper into the complexities that govern our spiritual direction in life. As we embark on this journey together, I ask Allah SWT to make this work a means for you to get closer to Him so that you may worship Him devoutly and fulfil the purpose of your very existence.

With sincerity and humility, I invite you to embark on this unusual journey, where the wisdom of duality unfolds, revealing the profound beauty and sophistication of Allah's creation.

May Allah SWT bless our journey and grant us wisdom, insight and increase us in knowledge. *Amīn*.

INTRODUCTION

Night and Day: Exploring the Wisdom of Duality

What a beautiful life, what a blessed life that was given by Allah SWT! As we go on living on Earth by the will of Allah SWT, we are perpetually in awe by the beauty found within the Qur'anic revelation and the teachings of our beloved Prophet Muhammad SAW. A thrilling aspect lies in the profound grasp of dualities, which softly influence both our universe and our lives. The delicate balance between light and darkness, good and evil, joy and sorrow, love and hate reflect a higher wisdom guiding all existence. Anyone gifted with such an insightful perspective, is inspired to contemplate life's complexities and beauties.

"***Night & Day***" explores the concept of divine pairs in our lives, as seen through the Islamic primary sources, traditions and teachings. The purpose is to deeply look at the delicate balance between these opposing forces, crafted, fashioned and designed by Allah SWT, *al-Badīʿ*—the most Exquisite and Magnificent Creator.

Within the essence of creation, we discover these pairs as the defining fabric of our very existence. There is not a single person who does not struggle between good and evil, or even the obvious contrasts like Angels and Satan. Luckily, we are not alone in this hardship, the Qur'an and sunnah are there to guide us through positives and negatives, ultimately shaping our reality in this world. Additionally, they play an essential role in shaping our eternal destination in the Hereafter, leaving a mark on every aspect of our lives. There is a wealth of wisdom to be found behind these dualities through careful exploration and analysis. By doing so, we enrich the very understanding of the purpose and meaning of our existence.

Exploring Duality:

The dualities go beyond mere theoretical ideas; they represent an attuned balance created by SWT. But why do these opposing forces exist? Is there any higher purpose to it? Let me be your humble guide throughout this book's journey in shedding light to concepts like compassion and retribution, life and death, creation and destruction etc., through the Qur'an and the teachings of our beloved Prophet SAW.

These contrasting elements provide valuable perspectives that influence how we perceive our own existence. And so, through the exploration of dualities, we gain a deeper idea of the interconnectedness and balance within the universe and its relation to our own spiritual journey.

For Seekers of Knowledge:

Are you eager to expand your knowledge and delve deep into the complex understanding that shapes your spiritual direction in life? Seek no more, this book is the right invitation to individuals like you. As we embark on this journey of enlightenment and exploration, may our reverence for the harmonious creation of Allah SWT deepen and become more profound, as it is evident for all to see. *Amīn.*

Wael Ibrahim

CHAPTER 1
Light and Darkness

Our life embodies light and darkness, we can never quite hold on to one or escape the other. They are both related to us, essential to our inner and outer world, but how exactly can we read the two?, The distinction of **light** and **darkness** emerges as a profound metaphorical framework within the realm of the Qur'an's beautiful signs and in the guided teachings of our Prophet Muhammad SAW. Let this chapter be your comprehensive guide on exploring the symbolic significance attached to **light** and **darkness** in harmony with the Islamic sources.

What is this light our heart desires and what is this darkness that makes our heart tremble? **Light**—often synonymous with **goodness**, **guidance**, and **divine illumination**, stands in a clear contrast to **darkness**, which represents **ignorance**, **evil**, and **the absence of divine guidance**.

Light as Divine Illumination

The metaphor of light can often be found in the Qur'an, the ultimate source of guidance for mankind, to convey Divine wisdom, guidance, and illumination. In surah an-Nur (The Light), Allah SWT reveals the metaphorical importance of light:

> "Allah is the Light of the heavens and the earth. The example of His light is like a niche within which is a lamp, the lamp is within glass, the glass as if it were a pearly [white] star lit from [the oil of] a blessed olive tree, neither of the east nor of the west, whose oil would almost glow even if untouched by fire. Light upon light. Allah guides to His light whom He wills. And Allah presents examples for the people, and Allah is Knowing of all things."

(an-Nur, 24:35)

Now imagine how your whole being is filled with light just by reading this profound *ayah*. It paints a vivid picture of divine illumination and guidance, using the metaphor of 'light upon light' to emphasise the boundless nature of Allah's guidance and love for His creation. The analogy of a lamp within a niche signifies the protection and clarity that Allah's guidance offers. This would be similar to a radiant star lit from the blessed olive tree—an image that transcends all worldly imaginations and material.

The Prophet's Radiant Guidance: A Beacon in Darkness

Where should we seek a real-life manifestation of this guided light? The answer is simple, in the life of Prophet Muhammad SAW which has brought the believers to goodness and everlasting bliss. His character, actions, and teachings have illuminated the entire world, dispelling the darkness of ignorance and the idolatry of worshipping other than Allah SWT. Through the light of the Qur'an, he became a walking Qur'an.

Narrated by 'A'isyah RA, she said about the character of the Prophet SAW: "**His character was the Qur'an.**" (ṣaḥīḥ Muslim 746a) And what was the Qur'an exactly? Allah SWT stated:

> "O' mankind, there has come to you a conclusive proof from your Lord, and We have sent down to you a clear light."

(an-Nisa', 4:174)

> "And thus, We have revealed to you an inspiration of Our command [i.e., the Qur'an]. You did not know what is the Book or [what is] faith, but We have made it a light by which We guide whom We will of Our servants. And indeed, [O' Muhammad], you guide to a straight path."

(ash-Shura, 42:52)

This concise yet profound statement alone is sufficient for you to grasp—the idea that the Prophet Muhammad SAW embodied the teachings of the Qur'an in his daily life. His actions, decisions, and interactions with others reflected the divine light and guidance that he received as a messenger from Allah SWT. We should rejoice in having the most perfect example and the choice to live according to it.

Light as a Symbol of Guidance: Qur'anic Evidences

1. Guidance for Mankind:

Allah SWT describes the Qur'an as a book of guidance and light for humanity:

"Indeed, this Qur'an guides to that which is most suitable and gives good tidings to the believers who do righteous deeds that they will have a great reward."

(al-Isra', 17:9)

Some may see the Qur'an as merely a set of rules or a number of obligations. However, this could not be further from the truth. The Qur'an is also a source of grand illumination, guiding those who believe in Allah SWT towards what is most appropriate and rewarding.

2. Guidance Out of Darkness:

In surah al-'Ankabut, Allah SWT emphasises the transformative power of His guidance:

"O' My servants who have believed, indeed My earth is spacious, so worship only Me. Every soul will taste death. Then to Us you will be returned. And those who have believed and done righteous deeds—We will surely assign to them of Paradise [elevated] chambers beneath which rivers flow, wherein they abide eternally. Excellent is the reward of the [righteous] workers who have been patient and upon their Lord rely."

(al-'Ankabut, 29:56-59)

The believers' way out of the darkness of disbelief and ignorance is through the help of patience, the light of faith, and reliance on Allah SWT.

Darkness: The Result of Ignorance and Evil

What does Islam teach us about darkness? According to it, darkness is not merely the absence of physical light but a metaphorical realm symbolising ignorance, deviation from Allah's clear guidance, and the embodiment of evil and evil actions. The Qur'an uses the metaphor of darkness to depict various aspects of human behaviour and moral conduct.

1. Darkness as Ignorance:

What is the difference between those in darkness with those granted divine light? This is how Allah contrasts the two states:

"And is one who was dead and We gave him life and made for him light by which to walk among the people like one who is in darkness, never to emerge therefrom?..."

(al-An'am, 6:122)

On one hand, the metaphorical death refers to a state of spiritual ignorance and misguidance. On the other hand, the light symbolises guidance granted by Allah SWT towards the ultimate reward, *Jannah*.

2. **Evil Actions as Darkness:**

Darkness is related with the deeds of those who reject faith and engage in evil activities, Allah SWT stated:

> "And whoever turns away from My remembrance—indeed, he will have a depressed [i.e., difficult] life, and We will gather [i.e., raise] him on the Day of Resurrection blind. He will say, 'My Lord, why have you raised me blind while I was [once] seeing?' [Allah] will say, 'Thus did Our signs come to you, and you forgot [i.e., disregard] them; and thus, will you this Day be forgotten.'"
>
> (Ṭaha, 20:124-126)

The darkness of a depressed life and blindness on the Day of Resurrection symbolises the consequences of abandoning Allah's guidance and following the desires of this *dunya*.

The Battle of *Badr*: A Manifestation of Light and Darkness

The Battle of *Badr*, an epochal moment in Islamic history, unfolds a historical context of **light** and **darkness**, the two contrastive themes in true conflict with one another. This paints a great picture of heroism and adversity. The Muslims, with a humble force, fearlessly faced the powerful and oppressive Quraysh army. The night before the battle, the Prophet Muhammad SAW prayed repeatedly saying:

> "O' Allah! If You wish (to destroy the believers), You will never be worshipped after today."
>
> (Ṣaḥīḥ al-Bukhari 2915)

This earnest prayer signifies the spiritual struggle against the forces of darkness, ignorance, and oppression. Few were the Muslims' chances of success, but instead of falling into complete desperation, they turned to prayer. In the following battle the Muslims were favoured by divided forces. The power of their prayer alone was more potent than the power of the opposite army. This serves as a manifestation of the triumph of light over darkness, guided by the will of Allah SWT and His ultimate power. If prayers can work in such adversity, just think what they can do to your daily life.

Light and Darkness in Rituals: Ṣalah and Ramadan

1. *Ṣalah* as Illumination:

The daily act of worship and the most important of all is *Ṣalah*. It is considered to be the cornerstone of all acts of worship. How beautiful that we as believers can make use of this daily act to symbolise our connection with the divine guidance of Allah SWT to remain firm upon the Straight Path. That's why these were the precise words of the Prophet Muhammad SAW while going to the *masjid* for *Fajr* especially:

> "O' Allah, place light in my heart, light in my tongue, light in my hearing, light in my eyesight, light on my right hand, light on my left hand, light in front of me, light behind me, light below me, O' Allah, give me abundant light."
>
> (Sunan Abi Dawud 1353)

Engaging in *ṣalah*, even while we are blindly walking in the darkness, is what illuminates our hearts and ease our path to *Jannah*. In other words, do not find yourself discouraged in your darkness, there is always *ṣalah* to bring light into your life.

2. Ramadan: A Month of Light:

The blessed month of Ramadan is described by Allah SWT as a month full of guidance, which is undoubtedly one of the gifts that may lead the believers toward *Jannah*. Allah SWT stated:

> "The month of Ramadan [is that] in which was revealed the Qur'an, a guidance for the people and clear proofs of guidance and criterion…"

(al-Baqarah, 2:185)

This month is characterised by a heightened spiritual connection and a unique opportunity for believers to draw closer to the divine guidance of Allah SWT and His light. We should make use of this month, to grow closer to everything that is good. That is why, anyone who misses this opportunity is not seen in a good light. The Prophet SAW said:

> "May the man before whom I am mentioned - and he does not send salutations upon me - be humiliated. And may a man upon whom Ramadan enters and then passes, before he is forgiven, be humiliated. And may a man whose parents reached old age in his presence, and they were not a cause for his entrance to Paradise, be humiliated."

(Jamiʿ at-Tirmidhi 3545)

We can clearly see that there is no excuse for people to miss out on such an opportunity. The guidance—the Light of Allah SWT shines throughout the month of Ramadan inviting people to make things right, therefore, whoever ruins that is a loser.

Conclusion Striving towards the Light

Believers, within the beautiful religion of Islam, can find guidance in the metaphorical relationship of **light** and **darkness**. The Qur'an and the Sunnah of the Prophet Muhammad SAW consistently emphasise the transformative power of the divine light of Allah SWT. By doing so, they guide humanity away from the void of darkness characterised by ignorance, evil and worshipping other than the Creator Himself.

As believers, the quest for light becomes a spiritual journey—a journey to seek divine guidance, a quest that we always deeply seek in our *ṣalah*, (i.e. *as Ṣirāṭal Mustaqīm,* al-Fatiḥah, 1:6). This is highly apparent throughout the teachings of the Qur'an and was manifested in the radiant example set by our beloved Prophet Muhammad SAW. Therefore, taking into consideration all this provided help, it is now up to us as Muslims to constantly seek the guidance of Allah SWT i.e. the LIGHT, and to seek His protection from any type of DARKNESS, i.e. misguidance and evil ways.

May Allah SWT grant us light from all directions that will be bright enough to dispel the shadows of ignorance. May this light navigate the complexities of life with the radiance of iman until we find solace, peace and tranquillity in this world, as well as the Hereafter. May we all wholeheartedly embrace this light until we end up in Jannatul Firdaus. Amīn.

A verse to remember, learn by heart and apply if possible:

> "Allah is the Light of the heavens and the earth. The example of His light is like a niche within which is a lamp..."
>
> (an-Nur, 24:35)

What about your thoughts?

CHAPTER 2
Life and Death

We certainly cannot discuss opposites that surround our lives without bringing up the concepts of **life** and **death**. Something that occupies a central place within our faith and even those with different faith backgrounds. All humans, regardless of their differences, often get to ponder about these two.

It is important for us to reflect on the transient nature of our existence and the vast journey that extends beyond the boundaries of this world. As this is something we cannot escape, this chapter will be delving into the Islamic perspective of **life** and **death**. It will thoroughly explore the divine gift of life and the inevitable transition to the afterlife—a journey that connects this world and what we can observe now to the Hereafter and what is yet to come. So, let's dive in.

Life: A Divine Gift-Test and an Opportunity

Life, according to Islam, is a divine gift bestowed upon humanity by Allah SWT, our Creator and a test for all of us to do that which Allah SWT commanded and intended. We were granted such a precious gift so we can grow as individuals, enrich our minds and polish our thoughts, so that we might get the treasure of ending up in a better place in the Hereafter. The Qur'an acknowledges the sacredness of human life and the diversity of existence as signs of Allah's creative power. Just take a moment to reflect and truly see the immense creativity and beauty in every aspect of our existence, all crafted by our Creator, Allah SWT. The concept of life in Islam extends beyond mere biological existence; it encompasses the spiritual, moral, and ethical dimensions of human existence as well.

1. **Life as a Test:**

   We as Muslims stand here to be tested. The Qur'an repeatedly emphasises that life is a test, a fleeting opportunity for human beings to show their faith and obedience to Allah SWT:

> "[He] who created death death and life to test you [as to] which of you is best in deeds…"

(al-Mulk, 67:2)

Life, in this context, becomes a transient phase during which individuals are tested based on their actions and adherence to Allah's divine guidance. However, it is an honour to be bestowed upon such a test, to devote our existence to the One who granted it in the first place.

Life's test is dynamic and multifaceted, encompassing various dimensions such as moral conduct, social interactions, personal development and certainly, above all else, your relationship with Allah SWT. So, it is important to be careful in all of your relationships, the one with yourself, others and mostly, the one with Allah SWT.

2. Responsibility for Actions:

Islam teaches that every individual is accountable for their deeds in this life. We are responsible for everything that we do, be it its goodness or its opposite. The choices made, the actions performed, and the impact on others—all contribute to one's record of deeds:

> "So whoever does an atom's weight of good will see it, and whoever does an atom's weight of evil will see it."

(al-Zalzalah, 99:7-8)

The consequences of one's actions are acknowledged, underscoring the responsibility each person carries during their earthly and temporary life.

The more diverse our human experiences and circumstances, the more layers added to that test. This requires us as individuals to navigate challenges with patience, gratitude, trust in Allah SWT and His wisdom, and our obedience to ethical principles and values.

3. **Life as a Spiritual Journey:**

Life, as understood under the Islamic lenses, is not solely about the physical and material aspects. It is a spiritual journey wherein believers strive to draw closer to Allah SWT through worship, gratitude, and righteous living:

> "And I did not create the jinn and mankind except to worship Me."
>
> (adh-Dhariyat, 51:56)

The purpose of life, according to this verse, is centred around worship—a holistic concept embracing all aspects of a believer's existence. This means that we exist, first and foremost, to worship Allah SWT. Such a spiritual quest involves continuous self-reflection, repentance, and a conscious effort to align one's actions with Allah's divine guidance.

Death: A Transition to the Afterlife

Is death the end? In Islam, death is not viewed as an endpoint but as a transition—a journey from the temporal realm to the eternal afterlife. The Qur'an depicts death as an appointment that every soul will inevitably face:

> "Every soul will taste death, and you will only be given your [full] compensation on the Day of Resurrection. So he who is drawn away from the Fire and admitted to Paradise has attained [his desire]. And what is the life of this world except the enjoyment of delusion."
>
> (ali-'Imran, 3:185)

1. Preparation for the Hereafter:

Let us view the transient nature of life as a constant reminder to prepare ourselves as believers for the Hereafter. We might feel intense discomfort just by reading about this transition. We cannot help but fear death, although it is not to be feared if you have attained enough *taqwa* during your lifetime. Death should only be seen as a gateway to the eternal consequences of one's deeds:

> "And the worldly life is not but amusement and diversion; but the home of the Hereafter is best for those who fear Allah, so will you not reason?"
>
> (al-An'am, 6:32)

This life on Earth is but a play, an amusement, a delusion. It is pivotal to truly grasp the temporary nature of all worldly pleasures because it encourages the believers to prioritise their actions in accordance with the principles of piety. We should not forget that there is something beyond, something bigger than our ordinary lives here.

Preparing for the Hereafter involves a conscious effort to adhere to the Islamic teachings as found in the Qur'an and the sunnah of the Prophet SAW, seeking forgiveness for our shortcomings, and engaging in acts of charity and benevolence to the best of our ability. We must strive to be the highest version of our believer selves, to make the most of this preparation for the Hereafter. After all, this is why we are here.

2. The Journey to the Hereafter:

What happens after death? It is the beginning of the soul's journey to the afterlife since death is portrayed as the departure from this earthly life.'. Death is among the most difficult topics for humans to talk about. Let alone imagining one's own death, that is indeed terrifying. Yet, the Prophet Muhammad SAW encouraged us to remember it often. He said:

> "'Frequently remember the destroyer of pleasures,' meaning death."
>
> (Sunan ibn Majah 4258)

Why should we ponder on such a 'destroyer of pleasures'? Remembering death, though scary and worrying, brings our attention to the reality of this life. It reminds us that one day we will be standing before Allah SWT for what we have done throughout our journey in this *dunya*.

The Prophet SAW emphasises the transient nature of the worldly pleasures and the importance of maintaining a balance between the material and spiritual aspects of life. In thinking about death, we are constantly aware of these truths.

3. Barzakh: The Intermediary Stage or Barrier between Death and the Day of Judgement:

Islam teaches us that after death, there is an intermediate stage known as *Barzakh* or a waiting period, where the soul experiences a different reality before the Day of Resurrection:

> "…and behind them is a barrier until the Day they are resurrected."
>
> (al- Mu'minun, 23:100)

Barzakh is a realm where souls await the final judgement, and their deeds are weighed for accountability. This concept emphasises the continuity of the soul's existence beyond the physical demise, reinforcing the idea that **death is not the end but a transition to another phase of existence**. This idea helps us make peace with the rather scary realities of death.

The Soul: A Divine Trust

Life is a gift and an opportunity that we all possess, yet how much do we actually know about it? Islam, being a very comprehensive way of life, emphasises throughout its teachings that human life is a union of body and soul. It is an enchanting combination of both, we are more than just our physical bodies. We should not forget that we possess the soul as well, in order to nurture it too. The soul and the body are considered to be a trust from Allah SWT until the Day of Judgement. Though the body vanishes on earth after death, the soul continues its journey beyond the confines of earthly existence (*"Every soul will taste death..."* — ali-'Imran, 3:185). The Qur'an describes the creation of humans and the infusion of the soul as a particularly special act of Allah SWT:

> "So when I have proportioned him and breathed into him of My [created] soul, then fall down to him in prostration."
>
> (Ṣad, 38:72)

1. The Nature of the Soul:

We keep hearing of the soul, yet at times people view it as something distant. It is not so; our soul is our very essence. More precisely, the soul, originating from Allah SWT Himself, represents the spiritual essence of an individual. It transcends the limitations of the physical body and can never be entirely explained by any human:

> "And they ask you, [O' Muḥammad], about the soul. Say, 'The soul is of the affair [i.e., concern] of my Lord. And you [i.e., mankind] have not been given of knowledge except a little.'"
>
> (al-Isra', 17:85)

It might be this little knowledge that people shy away from discussing. The nature of the soul remains a profound mystery, known only to Allah SWT.

Muslim scholars have delved into discussions about the nature of the soul, its connection to the body, and the intricacies of its existence etc. However, they would always use the above verse as their point of reference, which clearly states that only very little knowledge of the soul has been given to us.

2. Accountability of the Soul:

The soul is entrusted with free will and the ability to make choices. It will be held accountable for its deeds, and the consequences will be determined in the afterlife:

> "On the Day a man will flee from his brother, and his mother and his father, and his wife and his children, for every man, that Day, will be a matter adequate for him."
>
> ('Abasa, 80:34-37)

Even as deeds are taken into consideration, the individuality of the soul endures, reflecting its singular journey and personal responsibility.

The concept of accountability highlights the significance of conscious decision-making and moral responsibility in the journey of the soul. In other words, we need to treasure our soul in harmony with the teachings of our faith.

3. The Spirituality of the Soul:

The journey of the soul is inherently linked to spiritual development. The soul is drawn towards both good and evil, the Qur'an describes, urging individuals to purify and elevate their souls through conscious effort:

"And [by] the soul and He who proportioned it. And inspired it [with discernment of] its wickedness and its righteousness, He has succeeded who purifies it, And he has failed who instils it [with corruption]."

(ash-Shams, 91:7-10)

The soul on its own is not entirely good or entirely bad, it is rather a blending of both. Due to such innate nature that includes both **positive** and **negative** inclinations, it is up to the individual's choices to determine the soul's state.

How to keep the soul pure? **Acts of worship, reflection,** and **adherence to ethical principles** contribute to the soul's purification and spiritual elevation. To put it simply, we can train our souls toward what is pleasant and acceptable by He who created it. In the same light, we can guide it in the opposite direction. The choice will always be yours. You have the power to decide between purifying the soul or staining the soul. Choose wisely.

The Eternal Significance

Life and *death* are integral components of the plan designed by Allah SWT, in the grand narrative of the Islamic teachings. On one hand, life is a divine gift, a test of faith and obedience, and an opportunity for individuals to fulfil their purpose in this life. Death, on the other hand, is a transition to the afterlife—a continuation of the soul's journey into eternity.

What is the worth of knowing about the concepts of life and death or even the soul? Understanding the temporal nature of life inspires the believers to prioritise their actions and strive for righteousness. Death, though frigthening, should be embraced and accepted as a natural phase in the divine scheme of existence. The soul, as a divine trust, bears the responsibility of its choices, and the afterlife becomes the realm where the consequences unfold.

The complexities of life can often overwhelm believers because they are not easy to tackle. Fortunately, the concepts of life and death provide an elaborative framework for understanding the purpose of existence.

May Allah SWT grant us the right understanding and shower us with His Mercy during our time on earth. May He do so when we meet Him on the Day of Judgement with the purest of all hearts. *Amīn*.

A verse to remember, learn by heart and apply if possible

"And the worldly life is not but amusement and diversion; but the home of the Hereafter is best for those who fear Allah, so will you not reason?"

(al-An'am, 6:32)

What about your thoughts?

CHAPTER 3
Mercy and Wrath

Mercy and Wrath stand as pillars whenever the discussion of religion is raised, especially in Islam. If the two are still unclear to you, do not trouble your mind. This chapter delves into the profound understanding of Allah's Mercy and Wrath and will illuminate these concepts to any reader by Allah's will. It will explore the all-encompassing nature of the Divine Mercy and the consequences of straying from the righteous path that He intended for His creation.

Allah: The Most Merciful

1. Ar-Raḥmān and ar-Raḥīm: The Incomparable Mercies of Allah SWT:

Allah SWT is described in the Qur'an with the attributes of *ar-Raḥmān* (the Most Merciful) and *ar-Raḥīm* (the Most Compassionate). These attributes emphasise the vastness and incomparability of His mercy. Such unmatched mercy brings peace to the heart of the believer. From verse ONE and throughout the Qur'an we read:

"In the name of Allah, the Most Gracious, the Most Merciful."

(al- Fatiḥah, 1:1)

The opening verse of the Qur'an begins by acknowledging Allah's boundless mercy, setting the tone for the entire message of His Noble Book.

2. Mercy as a Fundamental Attribute:

The mercy of Allah SWT goes beyond being just an attribute, it is rather a fundamental aspect of His nature. It precedes all actions and encompasses all creations:

"...but My mercy encompasses all things…"

(al-Aʿraf, 7:156)

This verse brings into attention the universality of Allah's mercy, embracing every aspect of His creation.

3. Creation as an Act of Mercy:

What is better than the creation itself to express Allah's mercy? In a hadith *Qudsi*, Allah SWT declared upon perfecting His creation:

> "When Allah had finished His creation, He wrote over His Throne: 'My Mercy preceded My Anger.'"
>
> (Ṣaḥīḥ al-Bukhari 7422)

Are you afraid that you have sinned to the point that all bridges to our Creator have been burned? That your deeds are not in line with the teachings of Islam, therefore there are infinite distances between you and the Divine? Do not lose hope believers because Allah's Mercy and Kindness are still close to you, always.

4. Guidance as a Mercy:

If you feel lost and astray, there is always the Qur'an to bring direction into your life. The Qur'an is often referred to as a mercy and a guidance for humanity. It provides a roadmap for righteous living and a means of seeking Allah's mercy:

> "O' mankind, there has to come to you instruction from your Lord and healing for what is in the breasts and guidance and mercy for the believers."
>
> (Yunus, 10:57)

Allah SWT is reminding us that the Qur'an serves not solely as a book of commands, but as a guiding light and a source of mercy as well.

Not only that, but the man entrusted with delivering the Qur'an, Muhammad SAW, is depicted in the same Qur'an as a mercy to the entire creation:

"And We have not sent you, [O' Muhammad], except as a mercy to the worlds."

(al-Anbiya', 21:107)

The mission of Prophet Muhammad SAW is described as an act of mercy, highlighting the role of the divine guidance in humanity's salvation by sending them a merciful messenger.

The Concept of Allah's Wrath

1. Justice and Wrath:

While Allah is infinitely merciful, His justice is also emphasised. There is the need for Allah's wrath in order to apply and maintain justice and accountability on earth and in the Hereafter:

"Indeed, Allah orders justice and good conduct and giving [help] to relatives and forbids immorality and bad conduct and oppression. He admonishes you that perhaps you will be reminded."

(an-Nahl, 16:90)

Do you wish to be in Allah's favour and rejoice in His *Jannah*? There is nothing dearer to one's heart than that. All you need to do is remain consistent in your righteous actions to the best of your ability. It is especially significant to be just and morally right for as long as we are alive.

2. Warnings and Consequences:

It is not rare that believers forget about what is truly important in their temporary lives. The Qur'an warns about the consequences of deviating from the righteous path into the opposite destination. These warnings are an expression of Allah's justice and a reminder of the awaiting accountability:

"And let not those who [greedily] withhold what Allah has given them of His bounty ever think that it is better for them. Rather, it is worse for them. Their necks will be encircled by what they withheld on the Day of Resurrection. And to Allah belongs the heritage of the heavens and the earth. And Allah, with what you do, is [fully] Aware."

(ali-'Imran, 3:180)

If today you are not sharing or making use of Allah's blessings, you will most certainly account for it on the Day of Resurrection. A clear reminder of the Divine justice because of what you held back, never truly belonged to you in the first place.

3. Balancing Mercy and Wrath:

The Qur'an emphasises the balance between Allah's mercy and His occasional wrath. While mercy is abundant, the consequences of wrongdoing are also clear and cannot be ignored:

"...but My mercy encompasses all things. So I will decree it [especially] for those who fear Me and give zakah and those who believe in Our verses."

(al-A'raf, 7:156)

How to best receive His mercy? Put your focus on the fear of Allah SWT, known as *taqwa*, do charitable deeds, and adhere to His commands to the best of your ability. This highlights the balance between the Divine mercy and accountability for our actions.

The Mercy of Allah in Daily Life

1. Seeking Repentance:

Allah's mercy is perpetually inviting you for repentance. It is never too late; your sins are never too great, for Allah SWT is greater than anything and everything. The Qur'an encourages the believers to turn to Allah SWT in repentance, regardless of the nature of their sins:

"Say, 'O' My servants who have transgressed against themselves [by sinning], do not despair of the mercy of Allah. Indeed, Allah forgives all sins. Indeed, it is He who is the Forgiving, the Merciful.'"

(az-Zumar, 39:53)

Can you read the above again? Are you still afraid that you will not be able to receive forgiveness from Allah SWT because of your grave sins? Did you wrong others and even yourself? There is still the light of hope that shines upon the darkness of sins, so despair not. The limitless nature of Allah's forgiveness will embrace you back home. All you need to do is seek repentance and return to Him in obedience.

2. Compassion towards Others:

The teachings of the Prophet Muhammad SAW are the embodiment of mercy. His character and actions serve as the ultimate model for the believers in treating others with compassion. Allah SWT states, as quoted earlier:

"And We have not sent you, [O' Muhammad], except as a mercy to the worlds."

(al-Anbiya', 21:107)

Prophet Muhammad's mission was depicted in the aforementioned verse as a mercy to all of Allah's creation, underlining the universal and timeless essence of his message.

Are you selective in offering your mercy and kindness to others? The Prophet Muhammad SAW urged us to show mercy to one and all. It does not matter who they are or what their background is. He SAW declared:

> "The merciful are shown mercy by ar-Raḥmān. Be merciful on the earth, and you will be shown mercy from Who is above the heavens. The womb is named after Ar-Raḥmān, so whoever connects it, Allah connects him, and whoever severs it, Allah severs him."

(Jamiʿ at-Tirmidhi 1924)

As can be seen here clearly, the concept of mercy is part of our daily interactions among the Muslims and other segments of the society as well.

Balancing Hope and Fear

1. Hope in Allah's Mercy:

Islam encourages us to have hope in Allah's mercy, even in the face of sin and wrongdoing. The Prophet SAW said:

> "Allah is more pleased with the repentance of a servant as he turns towards Him for repentance than this that one amongst you is upon the camel in a waterless desert and there is upon (that camel) his provision of food and drink also and it is lost by him, and he having lost all hope (to get that) lies down in the shadow and is disappointed about his camel and there he finds that camel standing before him. He takes hold of his nose string and then out of boundless joy says: O Lord, Thou art my servant and I am Thine Lord. He commits this mistake out of extreme delight."

(Ṣaḥīḥ Muslim 2747a)

The imagery of finding a lost camel in the desert symbolises the intense joy of repentance and Allah's boundless mercy when we find our way back to Him, demonstrating our sincerity and humility upon our return.

2. Fear of Allah's Wrath:

Simultaneously, believers are encouraged to maintain a healthy fear of Allah's wrath and punishment, so you recognise the consequences of disobedience:

> "And those who [carefully] maintain their prayer: They will be in gardens, honoured. So what is [the matter] with those who disbelieve, hastening [from] before you, [O' Muhammad], [to sit] on [your] right and [your] left in separate groups? Does every person among them aspire to enter a garden of pleasure? No! Indeed, We have created them from that which they know. So I swear by the Lord of [all] risings and settings that indeed We are able to replace them with better than them; and We are not to be outdone."

(al-Maʿarij, 70:34-41)

Do we all wish to enter the pure gardens and remain with pure hearts? Certainly. Thus, believers, be careful in who you keep close to you. You do not wish to suffer the fate of the ones who will not get to taste the joys of these gardens. The imagery of the believers in gardens and the contrasting fate of the disbelievers serves as a reminder of the consequences of one's choices.

The Harmonious Dichotomy

The concepts of **Mercy** and **Wrath** present a balanced dichotomy that encompasses the nature of Allah SWT. His mercy—vast and infinite—is an invitation for everyone to seek His forgiveness, turn to Him in repentance, accept His *deen*, and be compassionate in all their human relationships. At the same time, the reality of the Divine justice and wrath remains, reminding us of the importance of accountability and adherence to the righteous path.

As you, true believers, tread on the complex paths of life, make use of Allah's Mercy and Wrath as a guiding principle. It inspires hope, encourages repentance, and motivates compassionate interactions with others. Simultaneously, it instills a sense of responsibility, fear of deviating from the righteous path, and mindfulness of the consequences of one's own actions.

May Allah SWT deepen our understanding of His attributes and inspire us to live an enriched life that reflects both hope in His mercy and fear of His justice and punishment. *Amīn.*

Night & Day : Exploring the Divine Wisdom in Duality

A verse to remember, learn by heart and apply if possible:

"...and My mercy encompasses all things..."

(al-Aʿraf, 7:156)

What about your thoughts?

CHAPTER 4
Creation and Destruction

The will of Allah SWT.

When I was trying to shift from where I was in life to where I am today, it was one of these concepts that attracted my attention to Islam. This chapter will focus on the Islamic perspective on **creation** as an act of Allah's will and the concept of **destruction** as a consequence of disobedience and/or our own actions and decisions. The discussion will revolve around exploring the role of creation in illustrating the magnificence of Allah SWT, the Creator and the consequences of deviating from His path.

Allah SWT: The Supreme Creator

1. **Creation as an Act of Will:**

    The Qur'an repeatedly reinforces the notion that Allah SWT is the Creator of everything in the heavens and the earth. The act of creation is a manifestation of His Divine will:

    "Originator of the heavens and the earth. When He decrees a matter, He only says to it, 'Be,' and it is."

    (al-Baqarah, 2:117)

    He does not need much to create anything. The mere command of "**Be**" from Allah SWT brings into existence whatever He wills, highlighting the immediacy and simplicity of His creative power.

2. **Everything Subject to His Will:**

    Everything within the teachings of Islam affirms that the entirety of this amazing universe is subject to Allah's will. The heavens, the earth, and all that lies between them are under His control and command:

> "Say, 'He is Allah, [who is] One, Allah, the Eternal Refuge. He neither begets nor is born, nor is there to Him any equivalent.'"
>
> (al-Ikhlaṣ, 112:1-4)

Let us shed light to the oneness of Allah SWT together with His eternal nature, illuminating that He transcends the limitations of His creation.

3. Creation as a Sign of Allah's Power:

The diverse and sophistication of the created world are considered as signs pointing to the power and the wisdom of the Creator:

> "Indeed, in the creation of the heavens and the earth, and the alternation of the night and the day, and the [great] ships which sail through the sea with that which benefits people, and what Allah has sent down from the heavens of rain, giving life thereby to the earth after its lifelessness and dispersing therein every [kind of] moving creature, and [His] directing of the winds and the clouds controlled between the heaven and the earth are signs for a people who use reason."
>
> (al-Baqarah, 2:164)

The natural phenomena, the grandiosity of nature and the order in the universe all exist for us to see. May these signs inspire us into contemplation and recognition for the Creator.

Creation and Divine Wisdom

1. Purposeful Creation:

The creation of the heavens and the earth was not done as a random act—it was filled with purpose. Everything in the universe has a designated purpose and belongs to a larger meaningful plan:

> "And We did certainly create the heavens and earth and what is between them in six days, and there touched Us no weariness."
>
> (Qaf, 50:38)

In another verse, Allah SWT states:

> "And We did not create the heavens and earth and that between them in play."
>
> (al- Anbiya', 21:16 & ad-Dukhan, 44:38)

The concept of "six Days" is not to be understood as human days or 24 hours per day, but as distinct periods during which Allah SWT crafted the universe. Not only that He carefully fashioned it, but He did so with a purpose and not just for a jest.

2. Humanity as Vicegerents:

Human beings, in the process of Allah's creation, were appointed as vicegerents on earth, entrusted with the responsibility of fostering goodness and creating harmony on earth:

> "It is He who has made you successors upon the Earth…"
>
> (Faṭir, 35:39)

This verse considers humans as stewards, responsible for delivering the message of Allah SWT, the ethical dealings and the fair use of the resources and environment entrusted to them. In other words, just like how the world was crafted with purpose, we are also here for a very clear purpose.

3. Reflection in Creation:

The purpose of the created world is to serve as a means of reflection and a reminder of Allah's attributes. We are often encouraged in the Qur'an to ponder on the signs within the creation:

"Indeed, in the creation of the heavens and the earth, and the alternation of the night and the day, are signs for those of understanding-"

(ali-'Imran, 3:190)

Destruction as a Consequence

1. Destruction as Allah's Wrath:

While creation is an act of divine will, destruction can be a consequence of disobedience and transgression. The Qur'an describes instances of destruction as a result of divine wrath:

"And We had certainly given Moses guidance, and We caused the Children of Israel to inherit the Scripture as guidance and a reminder for those of understanding. So be patient, [O' Muhammad]. Indeed, the promise of Allah is truth. And ask forgiveness for your sin and exalt [Allah] with praise of your Lord in the evening and the morning. Indeed, those who dispute concerning the signs of Allah without [any] authority having come to them – there is not within their breasts except pride, [the extent of] which they cannot reach. So seek refuge in Allah. Indeed, it is He who is the Hearing, the Seeing."

(Ghafir, 40:53-56)

What happens when communities engage in disobedience and rejection of the divine guidance set by Allah SWT? More often than not, destruction.

2. Consequences of Transgression:

The Qur'an repeatedly narrates the stories of nations of the past that faced destruction due to their rejection of Allah's guidance and indulgence in sinful behaviours:

"And how many a city did We destroy while it was committing wrong—so it is [now] fallen into ruin—and [how many] an abandoned well and [how many] a lofty palace."

(al-Ḥajj, 22:45)

Do not be scared by such narratives because that is not the point. In truth, they only serve as warnings about the consequences of transgressing the limits set by Allah SWT. The smart one will avoid repeating the same mistake, and the foolish will dare to challenge Allah's limits. Decide for yourself, do you want to be the smart one, or the foolish one?

3. Natural Disasters and Divine Decree:

Natural disasters are NOT really natural. They are part of the calamities also viewed through the lens of Allah's divine order. While they may appear as destructive forces, we as Muslims must understand them as part of Allah's wisdom and plan:

"And with Him are the keys of the unseen; none knows them except Him. And He knows what is on the land and in the sea. Not a leaf falls but that He knows it. And no grain is there within the darknesses of the earth and no moist or dry [thing] but that it is [written] in a clear record."

(al-Anʿam, 6:59)

"...And We send not the signs except as a warning."

(al-Isra', 17:59)

The signs, including what is called natural disasters, are all around us. Do not disregard them, rather use their existence as a reminder and a warning to reflect on your actions and turn towards Allah SWT in repentance.

Seeking Protection and Refuge

1. Invocation for Protection:

Our beautiful religion, *alḥamdulillāh*, encourages us to constantly seek protection from Allah SWT against these forces. Various prayers (*du'a's*) exist in which the believers seek refuge in Allah's mercy and protection:

"Say, 'I seek refuge in the Lord of daybreak. From the evil of that which He created. And from the evil of darkness when it settles. And from the evil of the blowers in knots. And from the evil of an envier when he envies.'"

(al-Falaq, 113:1-5)

There are an abundance of other *du'a's* taught by the Prophet SAW that are meant to plea for protection. Some examples are listed below:

"Bismillāhil-ladhī la yaḍurru ma'asmihi syai'un fīl arḍi wa lā fīs-samā'i wa huwas sami'ul 'alīm"

(In the Name of Allah with Whose Name there is protection against every kind of harm in the earth or in heaven, and He is the All-Hearing and All-Knowing.)

(Riyaḍ aṣ-Ṣaliḥin 1457)

"Allāhumma 'innī 'as'alukal 'afwa wal 'afiyata fīd dunyā wal ākhirah"

(O' Allah, I ask You for forgiveness and well-being in this world and the Hereafter.)

(Sunan ibn Majah 3871)

"A'udhu bikalimātillāhit tammāti min syarrimā khalaq"

(I seek refuge in the Perfect Word of Allah from the evil of what He has created.)

(Ṣaḥiḥ Muslim 2708a)

2. Balance of Hope and Fear:

To hope for creation or to fear destruction? Or both? The understanding of the concepts of **creation** and **destruction** in Islam nurtures a balanced approach of hope and fear. All Muslims are encouraged to be hopeful of Allah's mercy while being fearful of His justice and punishment:

"Say, 'Call upon Allah or call upon the Most Merciful [ar-Raḥmān]. Whichever [name] you call—to Him belong the best names…'"

(al-Isra', 17:110)

"And fear a Day when no soul will suffice for another soul at all, and no compensation will be accepted from it, nor will any intercession benefit it, nor will they be aided."

(al-Baqarah, 2:123)

These verses are a direct invitation to you, to call upon Allah SWT using His names and attributes, and to acknowledge His mercy. At the same time, they invite you to be aware of Him and his promises so you can recognise the consequences of disobedience.

Submission to The Divine Will of Allah SWT

In the comprehensive framework of our beautiful way of life, i.e. Islam, the concepts of **creation** and **destruction** serve as powerful reminders of Allah's omnipotence and divine will. Creation illustrates the magnificence of Allah SWT, the Creator, inviting us to contemplate and recognise His characteristics and attributes. Destruction, on the other hand, is portrayed as a consequence of disobedience and wrongdoing, as well as a reminder of Allah's justice.

As Muslims journey through this *dunya*, the understanding of creation and destruction will ultimately encourage us to display humility, reflection, and submission to Allah's will and commands. It is sufficient to observe the natural world which He has created, vastly rich in its diverse and interconnected elements, to witness the testament of wisdom and purpose inherent in Allah's design. Simultaneously, if we suffer the consequences of destruction, we are warned against deviation from the path of righteousness intended by Allah SWT for all humanity.

May Allah SWT grant us all a reflective mind to feel grateful for His beautiful creation and for making us part of it. May He make us mindful of the consequences of our own evil actions and help us to stay humble and submissive to His divine will. *Amīn*.

A verse to remember, learn by heart and apply if possible:

"Originator of the heavens and the earth. When He decrees a matter, He only says to it, 'Be,' and it is."

(al-Baqarah, 2:117)

What about your thoughts?

CHAPTER 5
Guidance and Misguidance

One day I was told, you either choose the path that leads to righteousness or to the pitfalls of straying from Allah's commands and will. Either guidance or its opposite. What will it be for you?

One of the most interesting subjects that I came to study in depth was the Islamic profound perspective on ***guidance*** as emanating from Allah SWT—the ultimate guide, and the risk of ***misguidance*** arising from human choices that deviate from the Straight Path of Allah's *deen*. Therefore, I want to use this chapter with the intention of exploring the sources of guidance and the consequences of abandoning the righteous path set by Allah SWT for His creation.

Allah: The Ultimate Guide

1. Allah as the Source of Guidance:

Without question, Islam firmly declares Allah SWT as the ultimate guide. The Qur'an, the principal foundation of our religion, repeatedly emphasises Allah's role as the guide for those who genuinely seek His guidance:

"Not upon you, [O' Muhammad], is [responsibility for] their guidance, but Allah guides whom He wills…"

(al-Baqarah, 2:272)

"That is the guidance of Allah by which He guides whomever He wills of His servants. But if they had associated others with Allah, then worthless for them would be whatever they were doing."

(al-An'am, 6:88)

> "Indeed, this Qur'an guides to that which is most suitable and gives good tidings to the believers who do righteous deeds that they will have a great reward."
>
> (al-Isra', 17:9)

If you truly wish to fulfil your heart, soul and mind, turn to the Qur'an and you will find the guidance provided by Allah SWT right there in front of your very eyes. Rest assured that by doing so, you will find the direction towards what is most suitable for your well-being, both in this life and the Hereafter.

2. The Prophets as Guides:

Do you ever find yourself alone and in doubt? Indeed, it is certainly not easy to live in the right way in today's world. However, believers were granted divine advice and instructions. Allah SWT, out of mercy and love for His creation, has appointed prophets and messengers throughout history to serve as guides for humanity. Their mission was to convey the divine message, exemplify righteous living, and lead people towards the path of obedience to Allah SWT. Allah SWT stated:

> "...You are only a warner, and for every people is a guide."
>
> (ar-Ra'd, 13:7)

No individual is forgotten—we all have an appointed guide, as long as we are willing to be helped. The above verse is precisely an indication of this, all people were told to follow Allah's guidance and were under His care. As for our beloved Prophet SAW, Allah SWT specifically says:

> "There has certainly been for you in the Messenger of Allah an excellent pattern for anyone whose hope is in Allāh and the Last Day and [who] remembers Allah often."
>
> (al-Aḥzab, 33:21)

The Prophet Muhammad SAW is specifically distinguished as an exemplary model with his teachings, deeds, and character, providing a source of guidance for those who wish to attain the highest levels of *Jannah*.

3. The Role of the Qur'an:

The Qur'an, being the final and complete revelation, is the primary source of guidance for Muslims. It encompasses guidance in matters of faith, ethics, law, and morality:

"And We have revealed to you, [O' Muhammad], the Book [i.e., the Qur'an] in truth, confirming that which preceded it of the Scripture and as a criterion over it. So judge between them by what Allah has revealed and do not follow their inclinations away from what has come to you of the truth…"

(al-Mai'dah, 5:48)

The Qur'an goes beyond a mere source of guidance, it is rather a methodology to distinguish truth from falsehood.

Human Responsibility and Free Will

1. Choice and Accountability:

While Allah SWT is the ultimate guide, humans have the free will and the capacity to make choices and take actions. It is still up to us if we wish to be guided rightly, or go astray. In Islam, the individual's responsibility for their actions and choices is clearly emphasised:

"Whoever does righteousness, it is for his [own] soul; and whoever does evil [does so] against it. And your Lord is not ever unjust to the servants."

(Fuṣṣilat, 41:46)

Whenever you are torn choosing between righteousness or wrongdoing, reflect on what each will bring to your life. The right path will personally nourish your life, whereas the wrong path will harm both you and the world around you. As we put it like this, the choice is not as complex anymore. Do you wish to purify your life or not? Ultimately, you will reap the fruits of each of your choices, whatever those may be. Allah's justice ensures that everyone is held accountable for their own deeds.

2. Invitation to Guidance:

Allah SWT, once again, out of love and mercy for His creation, makes a generous invitation to all humanity to accept the guidance offered through the Qur'an and the teachings of the prophets. The Qur'an repeatedly invites people towards that path of guidance:

> "And We have already created man and know what his soul whispers to him, and We are closer to him than [his] jugular vein. When the two receivers [i.e., recording angels] receive, seated on the right and on the left. He [i.e., man] utters no word except that with him is an observer prepared [to record]. And the intoxication of death will bring the truth; that is what you were trying to avoid."

(Qaf, 50:16-19)

Notice the closeness between Allah SWT and yourself, to every individual? Be aware of the recording of deeds by His angels, and the inevitability of facing the truth in the Hereafter—what more reminders of the guidance available to humanity do you need? You are always called upon guidance, all that is needed is to fully embrace the invitation.

3. Misguidance from Human Choices:

Misguidance, in the Islamic context, is not a predetermined fate. In truth, misguidance is a consequence of human choices and actions that deviate from the clear teachings of Islam. The Qur'an gives warnings for individuals who can go astray due to their own decisions:

"And [mention, O' Muhammad], when Moses said to his people, 'O' my people, why do you harm me while you certainly know that I am the messenger of Allah to you?' And when they deviated, Allah caused their hearts to deviate. And Allah does not guide the defiantly disobedient people."

(aṣ-Ṣaf, 61:5)

"And as for Thamud, We guided them, but they preferred blindness over guidance, so the thunderbolt of humiliating punishment seized them for what they used to earn."

(Fuṣṣilat, 41:17)

In both verses above, we can see that the guidance of Allah SWT was provided to people. However, they refused to follow it and went on living with stubborn disobedience. Consequently, such misguidance was only intensified, all because of their own harmful choices.

The Qur'an as a Clear Guidance

1. Clarity of Guidance:

The Qur'an itself is considered as the ultimate guidance that distinguishes right from wrong. Open it and you will find verses that provide valuable instructions on matters of belief, worship, ethics, and interpersonal relations:

"Indeed, this Qur'an guides to that which is most suitable and gives good tidings to the believers who do righteous deeds that they will have a great reward."

(al-Isra', 17:9)

The Qur'an portrays each advices clearly, to ensure that the believers have a comprehensive roadmap for righteous living. In addition, it welcomes even the ones without faith, they can also make use of this invitation and grab it before it's too late.

2. Adherence to the Qur'an:

Islam is a religion of obedience, once you accept it as your faith, you are required to adhere to the guidance provided in the Qur'an as well as the teachings of the Prophet SAW. Deviation from this guidance is identified as a source of misguidance:

"And obey Allah (in this context, the Qura'n) and the Messenger (our Prophet, Muhammad SAW) that you may obtain mercy."

(ali-'Imran, 3:132)

Similarly, another verse expresses a form of warning related with those who might disobey Allah SWT and His messenger:

"And obey Allah and obey the Messenger and beware. And if you turn away - then know that upon Our Messenger is only [the responsibility for] clear notification."

(al-Ma'idah, 5:92)

"[Say], 'Then is it other than Allah I should seek as judge while it is He who has revealed to you the Book [i.e., the Qur'an] explained in detail?' And those to whom We [previously] gave the Scripture know that it is sent down from your Lord in truth, so never be among the doubters."

(al-An'am, 6:114)

The preceding verse invites people to recognise the clarity and truthfulness of the Qur'an and to avoid doubts that may lead them to misguidance.

3. **Consequences of Ignoring Guidance:**

The Qur'an also emphasises the consequences of ignoring or rejecting Allah's divine guidance. Misguidance results from the intentional turning away from the clear path:

"And whoever turns away from My remembrance—indeed, he will have a depressed [i.e., difficult] life, and We will gather [i.e., raise] him on the Day of Resurrection blind."

(Ṭaha, 20:124)

The portrayal of a depressed life and being resurrected as blind on the Day of Judgement highlights the spiritual and existential consequences of turning away from the clear guidance provided by Allah SWT. Remember, it is in your power to choose either this blindness, or to remain with light in the right path.

Seeking Guidance through Prayer

1. **The Role of Prayer (*Ṣalah*):**

Prayer, or our beautiful daily *ṣalah* is a fundamental practice within our religion. It serves as a means of seeking guidance, mercy, and closeness to Allah SWT. In addition to that, and as part of our submission to Allah's will, this is an obligatory duty upon every believer.

The opening chapter of the Qur'an, surah al-Fatiḥah, is recited in every unit of the prayer, underlining our need for guidance, as we plea in every *ṣalah*:

"Guide us to the straight path - The path of those upon whom You have bestowed favour, not of those who have earned [Your] anger or of those who are astray."

(al-Fatiḥah, 1:6-7)

By reciting this surah in every unit of *ṣalah*, believers are constantly reminded of the need for guidance and the recognition of the straight path that is leading to *Jannah*.

2. Guidance as a Continuous Process:

Seeking guidance through prayer is not a one-time ritual, but rather an ongoing process so long as we remain alive. As Muslims, we are encouraged to turn to Allah SWT in prayer for guidance in various aspects of life:

"Your ally is none but Allah and [therefore] His Messenger and those who have believed—those who establish prayer and give zakah, and they bow [in worship]."

(al-Ma'idah, 5:55)

Prayer should be the most important and consistent aspect of your life as a believer. It is what brings you closer to Allah SWT and His guidance.

3. *Tawakkul* (Reliance on Allah):

Within Islam, reliance on Allah SWT (*Tawakkul*) is encouraged alongside practical measures and actions. Trusting in Allah's guidance is accompanied with sincere efforts to follow Allah's guidance and His commands:

"And rely upon Allah; and sufficient is Allah as Disposer of affairs."

(al-Aḥzab, 33:3)

The concept of *tawakkul* reinforces the understanding that while seeking guidance, believers must also be actively engaged in righteous actions. Thus, you should trust in this guidance as well as apply the practical deeds. The Prophet Muhammad SAW restated this idea in the following narration:

"If you were to put your trust in Allah as you should, you would be given provision like the birds: they go out hungry in the morning and come back with full bellies in the evening."

(Musnad Aḥmad 205)

The Struggle Against Misguidance

1. The Role of Knowledge:

Knowledge is the most crucial tool in fighting misguidance. Islam places a high value on acquiring knowledge, as it illuminates the path of guidance and helps distinguish truth from falsehood:

"...Say, 'Are those who know equal to those who do not know?'..."

(az-Zumar, 39:9)

The rhetorical question stresses on the distinction between those who possess knowledge and those who remain in a state of ignorance. Where would you prefer to be, enriched by knowledge or impoverished by ignorance?

2. **Avoiding Misguidance in Society:**

In Islam, it is a common understanding about the shared responsibility of society to avoid misguidance. Encouraging good and discouraging evil are principles that strive to nurture righteousness and prevent misguidance. Allah SWT states:

> "And let there be [arising] from you a nation inviting to [all that is] good, enjoining what is right and forbidding what is wrong, and those will be the successful."
>
> (ali-'Imran, 3:104)

A community that commits itself to promoting what is good and preventing what is harmful is the epitome of a successful one. We should all give our contributions in creating such a society.

3. **Humility and Repentance:**

Acknowledging one's vulnerability to misguidance and cultivating humility are crucial in the battle against deviation. Repentance (*tawbah*) is a pathway to returning to Allah SWT after realising one's mistakes:

> "....And turn to Allah in repentance, all of you, O' believers, that you might succeed."
>
> (an-Nur, 24:31)

Being a good believer involves constant work and conscious efforts toward the right way. The path to success is a constant cycle of seeking guidance, acknowledging shortcomings, and turning to Allah SWT in repentance.

Navigating the Path of Guidance

As discussed in this chapter, the concepts of **guidance** and **misguidance** were designed to illuminate the path towards righteousness and warning against the risks of deviation and sinful behaviours. Allah SWT—as the ultimate guide, provides comprehensive guidance through the Qur'an and the teachings of all the prophets. Nevertheless, human's free will introduces the potential for misguidance, emphasising the importance of constant vigilance and reliance on Allah SWT in all our actions.

It is really important for us as Muslims to understand that clarifying the concepts of guidance and misguidance nurtures humility, continuous self-reflection, and an unyielding commitment to seeking Allah's guidance in every part of our life. The Qur'an, as a clear and comprehensive source of divine wisdom, serves as a timeless guide for individuals and societies. Therefore, always firmly hold on to its commands and directions.

May Allah SWT guide us towards His obedience in this *dunya* and may He guide us towards *Jannatul Firdaus* in the Hereafter. *Amīn*.

A verse to remember, learn by heart and apply if possible:

"Indeed, this Qur'an guides to that which is most suitable and gives good tidings to the believers who do righteous deeds that they will have a great reward."

(al-Isra', 17:9)

What about your thoughts?

CHAPTER 6
Jannah and *Jahannam*

Paradise (*Jannah*) and Hellfire (*Jahannam*) are two realms that await humanity beyond the horizon of this temporal existence. As we embark on a quest of these contrasting destinations, we may delve into the vibrant imagery that paints ***Jannah*** as the ultimate abode of eternal bliss, and ***Jahannam*** as a cautionary destination for those who deviated from the path of righteousness.

Paradise (*Jannah*): The Unimaginable Eternal Bliss

1. Layers of Ecstasy:

Jannah unfolds as a multifaceted realm, unveiling layers of ecstasy and delight for those who tread the path of righteousness as commanded by Allah SWT. The Qur'anic verses weave a narrative of gardens beneath which rivers flow, promising believers an unending cycle of joy and renewal:

> "And give good tidings to those who believe and do righteous deeds that they will have gardens [in Paradise] beneath which rivers flow. Whenever they are provided with a provision of fruit therefrom, they will say, 'This is what we were provided with before.' And it is given to them in likeness. And they will have therein purified spouses, and they will abide therein eternally."
>
> (al-Baqarah, 2:25)

Within these layers lies a delight that goes beyond the confinement of our earthly experience. Such beauty cannot even be imagined. Our Prophet Muhammad SAW said regarding *Jannah*:

> "There will be bounties which no eye has seen, no ear has heard and no human heart has ever perceived."
>
> (Riyaḍ aṣ-Ṣaliḥin 1891)

2. Proximity to the Creator, Allah SWT:

The warmest joy of *Jannah* lies not only in its material pleasures prepared for the believer, but in the deep closeness to the One who created you and I—Allah SWT. The believers are promised the pleasure of being near to Allah SWT, an honour that surpasses any worldly delight. What an enchanting experience awaits us, never felt before. The Prophet Muhammad SAW explained this concept of seeing Allah SWT plainly in the following narration:

> "You will see your Lord on the Day of Resurrection as you see this full moon and you will have no difficulty in seeing Him."
>
> (Ṣaḥīḥ al-Bukhari 7434)

My brothers and sisters in Islam, *Inshā'Allāh*, you will make home in *Jannah*, you will marvel in wonder for as long as your heart desires. Surrounded by the beauty of our Creator, we will hope that such a precious moment will never come to an end. Say *Amīn*.

3. Desires Fulfilled Beyond Imagination:

Jannah is the realm where every righteous desire finds fulfilment. The Qur'anic promise highlights that the believers will be granted all their possible desires and even more, treasures they cannot yet imagine:

> "...and you will have therein whatever your souls desire, and you will have therein whatever you request [or wish]."
>
> (Fuṣṣilat, 41:31)

This encompasses not only the physical pleasures, but also the fulfilment of the deepest yearnings of the soul. As I mentioned earlier, our imagination is unable to paint such enchanting sights.

4. The Eternity of Bliss:

In stark contrast to the fleeting joys of this world, *Jannah* offers an eternal haven of bliss. The Qur'an emphasises the everlasting nature of the rewards, promising solace and hope to sincere believers:

"Say, 'Is that better or the Garden of Eternity which is promised to the righteous? It will be for them a reward and destination. For them therein is whatever they wish, [while] abiding eternally. It is ever upon your Lord a promise [worthy to be] requested.'"

(al-Furqan, 25:15-16)

Jannah is not a transient paradise; it is rather an eternal abode where the joyous journey knows no end. *SubḥānAllāh*. Aren't you now yearning for *Jannah*?

Hell (*Jahannam*): The Awful Destination

1. Layers of Unyielding Torment:

Jahannam, on the other side, unfolds with layers of unyielding torment, each more severe than the other. The Qur'an repeatedly cautions us of the intense suffering that awaits those who deviate from the path of righteousness and disregard the commands of Allah SWT:

"Allah has promised the hypocrite men and hypocrite women and the disbelievers the fire of Hell, wherein they will abide eternally. It is sufficient for them. And Allah has cursed them, and for them is an enduring punishment."

(at-Tawbah, 9:68)

2. Intense Heat and Scalding Waters:

Vivid metaphors depict the intensity of the torments and sufferings of the Hellfire. The Qur'an speaks of scalding water and a painful punishment resulting from habitual disbelief:

"...For them will be a drink of scalding water and a painful punishment because they used to disbelieve."

(al-An'am, 6:70)

Does this sensory imagery frighten you? Do feel the fear, such depiction aims to show the severity of the punishment, take it as a warning. Be aware of such potential torture, so it discourages you from repeating the same cycle of disobedience and sins. Otherwise, we should blame no one but ourselves.

3. Chains and Shackles of Despair:

Jahannam is a place where inhabitants are restrained in chains and shackles, symbolising the constriction and helplessness of those who rejected the guidance of Allah SWT. They had the chance in this *dunya* to follow His commands, yet they did not. Consequently, they will meet the most horrifying fate:

"Indeed, We have prepared for the disbelievers chains and shackles and a blaze."

(al-Insan, 76:4)

4. Perpetual Regret and Despair:

The Qur'anic narrative paints a haunting picture for the inhabitants of Hellfire who are in a state of perpetual regret and despair. As they become aware of the missed opportunities for righteousness, their remorse keeps growing:

"And they will approach one another, inquiring of each other."

(as-Saffat, 37:50)

"And they will be given to drink a cup [of wine] whose mixture is of ginger [From] a fountain within it [i.e., Paradise] named Salsabeel."

(al-Insan, 76:17-18)

All these repetitive reminders of the wonderful beauties of Paradise, all these heavenly sights being out of reach for the ones who did not live according to their faith. All the people who did not make use of the opportunities they had while living in this *dunya* are now filled with deep regret and despair.

Seeking Redemption through the Mercy of Allah SWT

1. The Mercy of the Most Merciful, Allah SWT:

Within the contemplation of *Jannah* and *Jahannam*, the Islamic teachings echo the everlasting mercy of Allah SWT. The door of repentance and forgiveness remains wide open to those who turn to Him sincerely:

"Say, 'O' My servants who have transgressed against themselves [by sinning], do not despair of the mercy of Allah. Indeed, Allah forgives all sins. Indeed, it is He who is the Forgiving, the Merciful.'"

(az-Zumar, 39:53)

Let go of your sinful life, no matter what your past deeds are, there is still hope. You can return to the peace granted by Allah's forgiveness. You are never too far away from the right path, there is encouragement and redemption for as long as you are still breathing.

2. The Equilibrium of Fear and Hope:

The Qur'anic discourse on Paradise and Hell encourages believers to maintain a healthy balance between the fear of Allah's punishment and hope in His mercy, as discussed in previous chapters. Both emotions are fundamental to the spiritual journey of the believers. The Prophet Muhammad SAW mentioned that Allah SWT said:

> "Indeed Allah Most High says: 'I am as My slave thinks of Me, and I am with him when He calls upon Me.'"
>
> (Jamiʿ at-Tirmidhi 2388)

The gracious mercy of Allah SWT is a source of hope to everyone. Believers are inspired by His generosity, but they are not the only ones. Anyone who fears the consequences of straying from that righteous path finds reassurance in His mercy.

3. The Reverberating Reminder of Mortality:

Islamic teachings emphasise the transient nature of life and the certainty of death. Reflecting on mortality becomes a powerful motivator for seeking salvation and avoiding the pitfalls leading to Hell:

> "Every soul will taste death, and you will only be given your [full] compensation on the Day of Resurrection…"
>
> (ali-'Imran, 3:185)

The reminder of death to both believers and non-believers is a wake-up call to the fleeting moments of our earthly existence. When one keeps hearing that they will 'taste death', they will start considering more on the decision to pursue righteousness.

The Eternal Symphony of Existence

I tell my children to dream of *Jannah*, because it stands as the culmination of the believer's journey, a reality of bliss and fulfilment that we need to internalise every moment of our earthly existence. It truly needs to become part of us. *Jahannam*, on the other hand, serves as a stark reminder of the consequences that unfold when the path of righteousness and obedience of Allah SWT is forsaken.

Contemplation over these eternal realms should serve as our compass in life, guiding actions and choices to either the right way or its opposite. The vivid descriptions in the Qur'an evoke a sense of awe, humility, and an immense awareness of the consequences of one's own deeds.

May Allah SWT grant us all *Jannah* and guide us to all deeds that will bring us closer to it. *Amīn*.

A verse to remember, learn by heart and apply if possible:

"Indeed the companions of Paradise, that Day, will be amused in [joyful] occupation-They and their spouses-in shade, reclining on adorned couches. For them therein is fruit, and for them is whatever they request [or wish]."

(Yasin, 36:55-57)

What about your thoughts?

CHAPTER 7
Knowledge and Ignorance

Guidance starts with knowledge, especially the knowledge of understanding about the nature of Allah SWT. Whereas the opposite—ignorance, may lead to chaos.

Allah SWT, the All-Knowing, bestows upon humanity the invaluable gift of knowledge. He urges them to seek wisdom and enlightenment in every opportunity they get. This chapter will be exploring the virtues of knowledge and the importance of seeking it, and unravelling the terrifying shadows cast by ignorance upon the path of truth.

Knowledge as Divine Illumination

1. **Allah, the All-Knowing:**

   The Qur'an resounds with the affirmation of Allah's omniscience, emphasising His role as the All-Knowing. His knowledge transcends the limitations of time and space, embracing the smallest details of existence. The verse, "***And with Him are the keys of the unseen; none knows them except Him…***" (al-An'am, 6:59), paints a vivid picture of the comprehensive nature of His divine knowledge. This recognition establishes the basis of believers' understanding. It lays the groundwork for their journey to understand the identity of Allah SWT, as well as His requirements and expectations, to be able to worship Him on His own terms.

2. **The Virtue of Acquiring Knowledge:**

   The pursuit of knowledge is not merely encouraged in Islam; it is deemed obligatory. The Prophet Muhammad SAW explicitly stated:

   "Seeking knowledge is obligatory upon every Muslim…"

   (Sunan ibn Majah 224).

This obligation is not confined to a specific stage in life but extends from the cradle to the grave. You are never too young to learn, the way you are never too old for it. The emphasis on knowledge as a duty fosters a culture of lifelong learning, urging Muslims to constantly seek intellectual growth and enrichment. Little wonder why the first word that was ever revealed in the Qur'an was *"Iqra"* or **READ**.

3. **Knowledge as a Path to Virtue:**

Knowledge, in Islam, is not a neutral concept, it is rather a transformative force that leads to virtue and righteousness. The Qur'an asserts:

"...Only those fear Allah, from among His servants, who have knowledge…"

(Faṭir, 35:28).

This close relation between knowledge and piety brings into attention the moral dimension of acquiring wisdom. ***True and beneficial knowledge*** is expected to shape the character of individuals, aligning their actions with ethical principles. That is why the Prophet Muhammad SAW used to sincerely plea for it, saying:

"O' Allah, I ask You for beneficial knowledge…"

(Sunan ibn Majah 925).

4. **The Connection between Knowledge and Worship:**

Worship in Islam is not a ritualistic exercise; it is an ***informed acknowledgement*** of the divine existence of Allah SWT and His right to be worshipped. The Qur'an urges the believers to know and understand the Oneness of Allah SWT:

"So know, [O' Muhammad], that there is no deity except Allah and ask forgiveness for your sin…"

(Muhammad, 47:19).

Knowledge and worship are not separated from one another, and this truth elevates the act of devotion towards Allah SWT. Our prayers go beyond being mere rituals, they foster a deep spiritual engagement with Allah SWT. It is always better to KNOW who you are devoting your life to.

Ignorance: The Veil that Shrouds Understanding

1. **The Dangers of Ignorance:**

    Ignorance is portrayed in the Qur'an as a perilous condition that harms understanding and veils the truth. The verse, ***"…Say, 'Are those who know equal to those who do not know?'…"*** (az-Zumar, 39:9), serves as a rhetorical question, highlighting the blunt contrast between those illuminated by knowledge and those who are shrouded in ignorance. Ignorance becomes a barrier to true comprehension, hindering individuals from grasping the essence of the divine guidance revealed by Allah SWT. This is where the peril of ignorance stands, it distances us from our Creator.

2. **Ignorance as a Breeding Ground for Misunderstanding:**

    The Qur'an warns against speaking without knowledge, cautioning against the breeding ground of misunderstanding and misconception. The verse, ***"And do not pursue that of which you have no knowledge…"*** (al-Isra', 17:36), underscores the accountability related to spreading ignorance and falsehood. This emphasis on intellectual responsibility serves as a call for precision in thought and speech, discouraging the distribution of baseless ideas. And yes, that includes whatever you may share on social media platforms.

3. **Ignorance as a Barrier to Unity:**

Ignorance can act as a frightening barrier to unity and harmony within societies. As can be seen, by remaining ignorant, you do not harm only yourself, but the entire society. The Qur'an encourages dialogue and knowledge-sharing to foster understanding among diverse communities. *Daʿwah* or sharing the message of Islam is based solely on this idea:

"O' mankind, indeed We have created you from male and female and made you peoples and tribes that you may know one another…"

(al-Ḥujurat, 49:13).

As is shown by this verse, knowledge brings people together, it breaks down the walls of ignorance and promotes a sense of shared humanity, regardless of one's colour, sex or nationality.

4. **The Role of Ignorance in Deviation:**

The Qur'an narrates instances where ignorance resulted in the rejection of the divine guidance established by Allah SWT and the perpetuation of wrongdoing. The verse, ***"And among them are unlettered ones who do not know the Scripture except [indulgement in] wishful thinking, but they are only assuming."*** (al-Baqarah, 2:78), emphasises the futility of conjecture in the absence of true knowledge. Ignorance becomes a catalyst for deviation, blinding individuals to the light of Allah's guidance.

The Balance: Seeking Knowledge with Humility

1. Humility in the Pursuit of Knowledge:

Islamic teachings highlight the importance of approaching the acquisition of knowledge with humility. Rejoice in the fruit of knowledge with a humble heart. The Qur'an encourages the believers to seek knowledge while recognising the vastness of what they do not know:

"...And say, 'My Lord, increase me in knowledge.'"

(Ṭaha, 20:114).

This verse represents the acknowledgement that genuine knowledge is an endless journey, and humility is the companion of true wisdom.

Another verse regarding how little we know in comparison to the vast knowledge of Allah SWT is:

"...And you [i.e., mankind] have not been given of knowledge except a little."

(al-Isra', 17:85)

2. The Dangers of Arrogance and False Pride:

Arrogance and false pride can accompany ignorance, harming the sincere pursuit of knowledge. The Qur'an warns us against such attitudes and calls for humility in the face of divine wisdom:

"And the servants of the Most Merciful are those who walk upon the earth easily, and when the ignorant address them [harshly], they say [words of] peace."

(al-Furqan, 25:63).

This verse is an example of the wise ones whose attitude is grounded in knowledge and humility. They will surely have to deal with the arrogant and ignorant—we cannot avoid such people on this earth, however, they respond with kindness and/or remain silent when they are confronted by them. The travellers of the path of knowledge do not trouble their minds with arrogance, nor do they argue with the ignorant. Be true in your wisdom, do not allow others to disturb your peace.

3. **The Islamic Legacy of Knowledge:**

Islamic history bears witness to a rich legacy of knowledge and scholarship. The Golden Age of Islam witnessed unparalleled advancements in various fields, including science, mathematics, medicine, and philosophy. The scholars of that era sought knowledge as a means of drawing closer to Allah SWT and contributing to the improvement of humanity. This historical perspective sheds light to the intrinsic connection between Islam and intellectual enlightenment.

4. **Contemporary Relevance:**

In the contemporary context, the pursuit of knowledge remains a cornerstone of our faith as Muslims. We are encouraged to engage with various branches of knowledge, from the sciences to the humanities, and to contribute positively to the betterment of society. And of course, on top of all of that, to enhance our knowledge about the *deen* of Allah SWT to the best of our abilities. This emphasis on contemporary relevance positions knowledge as a dynamic force that continues to shape the world in alignment with our Islamic principles and values.

The Radiance of Enlightenment

In navigating this interesting topic on knowledge and ignorance, Islam illuminates a path that leads humanity from the shadows of misunderstanding to the radiance of enlightenment. Allah SWT, the All-Knowing, warmly invites humankind, especially the believers, to seek knowledge as a means of drawing closer to Him and navigating the complexities of life with wisdom and proper direction.

May Allah SWT enhance our knowledge and grant us the wisdom to recognise ignorance so that we may avoid its path and evil destination. May Allah SWT inspire all of us, to be able to make a profound commitment to lifelong learning, humility, and the pursuit of truth. *Amīn*.

In the journey of seeking knowledge, I ask Allah SWT to help all the believers to find not only intellectual enlightenment but also spiritual elevation, to draw closer and closer to the divine light that dispels the shadows of ignorance. *Amīn ya rabb al-ʿĀlamīn.*

A verse to remember, learn by heart and apply if possible:

"...Say, 'Are those who know equal to those who do not know?'..."

(az-Zumar, 39:9)

What about your thoughts?

CHAPTER 8
Forgiveness and Retribution

To forgive or not to forgive? This is THE question.

In fact, this is one of the questions that often bother many people. Indeed, it is quite challenging to forgive the ones who might have caused you harm. However, such a concept defines the divine balance between justice and mercy as demonstrated by our Creator. Allah SWT, the Most Merciful, is oft-forgiving, is always inviting the believers to seek His forgiveness and paving their way for their redemption. Simultaneously, the notion of retribution underlines the aftermath of wrongdoing. Yet, even in the face of justice, Allah's boundless mercy remains inviting to those who sincerely repent and do better.

This chapter gives an insightful overview of the concepts of forgiveness and retribution in Islam.

Allah's Oft-Forgiving Nature

1. The Essence of Forgiveness:

Islam places forgiveness at the core of its moral framework. Allah's nature is described as Oft-Forgiving and Most Merciful. The Qur'an repeatedly points to this aspect, calling all the believers to seek forgiveness and turn towards the compassionate nature of Allah SWT:

"…And turn to Allah in repentance, all of you, O' believers, that you might succeed."

(an-Nur, 24:31)

"'…but My mercy encompasses all things…'"

(al-A'raf, 7:156)

These verses encapsulate the all-encompassing mercy of Allah SWT, One that is willing to accept anyone who sincerely repents.

Your sins might be grand, but His forgiveness is grander.

2. The Virtue of Seeking Forgiveness:

The Qur'an encourages us to seek forgiveness and turn towards repentance. This is the only way that can erase our past mistakes. The act of seeking forgiveness is more than merely a way to make amends, it is also a manifestation of humility and acknowledgement of human fallibility:

"...And seek forgiveness of Allah. Indeed, Allah is Forgiving and Merciful."

(al-Muzzammil, 73:20)

This virtue of seeking forgiveness is intertwined with the Islamic concept of *tawbah*, signifying a sincere turning back to Allah.

A side note:

-Forgiveness or Istighfar is to seek Allah's pardon for the sins that you have committed in the past.

-Repentance or Tawbah is to commit not to return back to the same sins in the future.

3. The Prophetic Model of Forgiveness:

The life of Prophet Muhammad SAW serves as a model of forgiveness and kindness. Even in the face of adversity, he showed a forgiving nature, embodying the teachings of the Qur'an:

> "So by mercy from Allah, [O' Muhammad], you were lenient with them. And if you had been rude [in speech] and harsh in heart, they would have disbanded from about you…"
>
> (ali-'Imran, 3:159)

This verse highlights the power of leniency, mercy and forgiveness in fostering unity and strengthening community bonds.

4. The Vastness of Allah's Forgiveness:

Islam emphasises on the vastness and expansive nature of Allah's forgiveness. The name of Allah SWT 'Oft-Forgiving' is not a mere descriptor of who He is, but also an invitation for the believers to approach Him with hope and optimism:

> "And whoever does a wrong or wrongs himself but then seeks forgiveness of Allah will find Allah Forgiving and Merciful."
>
> (an-Nisa', 4:110)

Muslims should find the greatest comfort in this expansive forgiveness as they realise that no sin is beyond redemption. All they need to do is be willing to make amends and have a change of heart.

Retribution: Consequences of Wrongdoing

1. Justice as a Command from Allah SWT:

While forgiveness is celebrated, Islam equally upholds justice as a fundamental principle within the *deen*. Retribution becomes a consequence of wrongdoing, aligning with the broader concept of divine justice:

> "And the retribution for an evil act is an evil one like it, but whoever pardons and makes reconciliation – his reward is [due] from Allah. Indeed, He does not like wrongdoers."
>
> (ash-Shura, 42:40)

As the verse tells us, the consequences for doing evil are harsh, yet there is still the option of being forgiven. Witnessing the principle of retribution tempered with forgiveness best demonstrates the balance of justice and mercy.

2. The Limits of Retribution:

Islam sets clear boundaries for retribution, emphasising proportionality and fairness. The Qur'an outlines the principle of *Qiṣaṣ*, or the law of equal retaliation, ensuring that retribution is just and measured:

> "And there is for you in legal retribution [saving of] life, O' you [people] of understanding, that you may become righteous."
>
> (al-Baqarah, 2:179)

This verse marks the ultimate goal of justice—that is, the fostering of righteousness and order within society.

3. The Role of Repentance in Averting Retribution:

Islam also emphasises the transformative power of repentance in averting the consequences of wrongdoing. Allah's mercy is open to those who sincerely turn back to Him in genuine repentance:

> "And hasten to forgiveness from your Lord and a garden [i.e., Paradise] as wide as the heavens and earth, prepared for the righteous."
>
> (ali-'Imran, 4:110)

Repentance becomes a shield against the full weight of

retribution, allowing believers to reconcile with Allah SWT and open a door for themselves to tremendous rewards. Repent from the depths of your heart and you will feel the truest sense of safety.

4. The Divine Wisdom in Retribution:

Retribution, in the Islamic framework, is not arbitrary but aligned with the wisdom of our Creator. The Qur'an suggests that even in retribution, there may be elements of goodness and a deeper wisdom known only to Allah:

> "...But perhaps you hate a thing and it is good for you; and perhaps you love a thing and it is bad for you. And Allah knows, while you know not."
>
> (al-Baqarah, 2:216)

This verse brings to our attention the fact that human perspective is highly limited and the need to trust in the wisdom of Allah SWT that governs retribution is truly essential.

The Intersection: Forgiveness and Retribution in Harmony

1. The Divine Equation:

The Qur'anic narrative weaves forgiveness and retribution into a harmonious equation, reflecting the divine balance between justice and mercy, as explained earlier:

> "...Our Lord, do not impose blame upon us if we have forgotten or erred. Our Lord, and lay not upon us a burden like that which You laid upon those before us. Our Lord, and burden us not with that which we have no ability to bear. And pardon us; and forgive us, and have mercy upon us…"
>
> (al-Baqarah, 2:286)

This prayer embodies a heart-warming plea for forgiveness and mercy while holding recognition for human fallibility, sinful tendencies and error.

2. The Power of Sincere Repentance:

Islam stands unique in its emphasis on the transformative power of sincere repentance in minimising the consequences of wrongdoing. The Qur'an and the sunnah of the Prophet SAW are full of emphatic verses and narrations regarding repentance, as means of seeking forgiveness, as well as a pathway to spiritual elevation:

> "And O' my people, ask forgiveness of your Lord and then repent to Him. He will send [rain from] the sky upon you in showers and increase you in strength [added] to your strength…"
>
> (Hud, 11:52)

This verse illustrates the link between sincere repentance and the divine blessings that follow. All you have to do is repent. Afterwards, showers of goodness will fall upon your life.

3. The Compassionate Nature of Divine Justice:

The Qur'anic depiction of divine justice is not devoid of compassion. Allah's justice is filled with mercy and love. This helps the believers find assurance even in the face of retribution because the essential divine purpose is benevolent:

> "…but My mercy encompasses all things…"
>
> (al-A'raf, 7:156)

This recurring theme is yet another reminder that divine justice is guided by the encompassing mercy of Allah SWT.

4. **The Role of Human Choices in Seeking Allah's Forgiveness:**

Islam highlights the fact that human beings are free to choose and determine the course of forgiveness and retribution. The Qur'anic narrative stresses that repentance and seeking forgiveness from Allah SWT are active choices that individuals can make:

> "And those who, when they commit an immorality or wrong themselves [by transgression], remember Allah and seek forgiveness for their sins—and who can forgive sins except Allah? — and [who] do not persist in what they have done while they know."
>
> (ali-'Imran, 3:135)

The verse above emphasises the conscious effort required to seek forgiveness and to turn away from wrongdoing. It is humane to make mistakes, however, as believers we should make sure to reflect on these errors and make an attempt to right the wrongs by repentance.

The Divine Justice and Mercy

Through the above teachings about **forgiveness** and **retribution** emerges the clarity and the wisdom of Allah's divine **justice** and **mercy**. Allah's oft-forgiving nature invites believers to seek redemption, while the principle of retribution reminds us of the consequences of wrongdoing. The Qur'anic narrative harmonises these seemingly divergent concepts, revealing a compassionate divine justice that considers the nuances of human choices and the transformative power of sincere repentance.

May Allah SWT enable us to understand the beautiful religion of Allah SWT and the wisdom behind retributions sometimes. May He grant us the ability to seek His forgiveness and accept us when we return to Him with sincere repentance. *Amīn.*

A verse to remember, learn by heart and apply if possible:

"And whoever does a wrong or wrongs himself but then seeks forgiveness of Allah will find Allah Forgiving and Merciful."

(an-Nisa', 4:110)

What about your thoughts?

CHAPTER 9
Prophets and their Opponents

The timeless struggle between Allah's divine guidance and human resistance is a recurring theme within the Qur'anic narrative. This showcases the complex dynamics that unfold between the prophets of Allah SWT and His messengers and their opponents. The Prophets SAW, selected by Allah SWT, are bestowed with the monumental task of guiding humanity along the path of righteousness. Nonetheless, together with this divine call, there emerged opposition—individuals or entities that stubbornly hindered the message, thereby challenging the fundamental essence of prophethood and the entire message of Allah SWT. This chapter offers an in-depth exploration of the profound interplay between the prophets of Allah SWT and their opponents, in the hope of granting lessons for us today so that we can pay attention to every command found in the Qur'an or taught by these noble prophets. Let this chapter inspire you towards a more rightful lifestyle, by Allah's will.

The Divine Commission of Prophets

1. The Role of Prophets in Islam:

Throughout the Qur'an, we are told that the prophets are the chosen agents of Allah SWT on earth, entrusted with the sacred duty of conveying Allah's divine guidance to humanity. The Qur'an articulates this role in the following verse:

> "And We sent not before you any messenger except that We revealed to him that, 'There is no deity except Me, so worship Me.'"

(al-Anbiya', 21:25)

In reality, the prophets transcend the role of mere conveyors of information; they are bearers of a transformative message that calls humanity to embrace monotheism and live virtuously following Allah's will, and the principles He laid on earth for His creation.

2. The Diversity of Prophets:

Islam recognises the variety of prophets who were sent to mankind, with a myriad of messengers sent to diverse communities throughout history. Each prophet represents a pivotal link in the chain of this same divine guidance, tailored to meet the specific needs and circumstances of their people:

"And We certainly sent into every nation a messenger, [saying], 'Worship Allah and avoid Ṭaghut.'..."

(an-Naḥl, 16:36)

This diversity underlines the universal nature of the prophetic message and its enduring relevance across different temporal and geographical contexts. Believers of all nations get the opportunity of receiving the same prophetic message. In a narration mentioned by the Prophet SAW, he indicated that about 124,000 messengers have been sent to mankind throughout history.

"Then We sent Our messengers in succession. Every time there came to a nation its messenger, they denied him, so We made them follow one another [to destruction], and We made them narrations. So away with a people who do not believe."

(al-Mu'minun, 23:44)

3. The Exemplary Lives of Prophets:

In Islam, the prophets of Allah SWT served not only as the conveyors of the divine message but also as the living embodiments of the principles they preached. Their lives stand as exemplars of moral conduct, resilience, and unwavering faith. 'A'isyah RA, the wife of our Prophet Muhammad SAW, for example, mentioned:

"Yazid ibn Yabnus said, 'We went to 'A'isyah and said, 'Umm al-Mu'minin, what was the character of the Messenger of

Allah, may Allah bless him and grant him peace, like?' She replied, 'His character was the Qur'an.'"

(al-Adab al-Mufrad, Book 14, Hadith 308)

The Challenge of Opposition

1. Human Resistance to Divine Guidance:

Opposition to the prophetic message emerges as a recurring theme within the Qur'anic narrative. Almost every prophet encountered resistance and animosity. This human resistance is a result of a variety of factors, including pride, ignorance, and a very solid attachment to all the worldly desires available to them. Allah SWT states:

"And they rejected them, while their [inner] selves were convinced thereof, out of injustice and haughtiness…"

(an-Naml, 27:14)

This verse highlights the diverse cultural, psychological, and spiritual aspects intrinsic to the nature of opposition encountered by the prophets of Allah SWT in almost every period and region.

2. The Tactics of Opponents:

The Qur'an outlines the diverse tactics employed by opponents in their stubborn efforts to undermine the messages of the prophets of Allah SWT. These tactics range from engaging in mockery and ridicule to outright rejection:

"And those who disbelieve say to those who believe, 'Follow our way, and we will carry your sins.' But they will not carry anything of their sins. Indeed, they are liars."

(al-'Ankabut, 29:12)

Opponents regularly engage in deceptive rhetoric with the intention of discouraging the believers from adhering to the path of divine guidance.

3. The Prophet Muhammad and the Meccan Opposition:

The life of Prophet Muhammad SAW stands as an enduring testament to prophetic perseverance amidst constant opposition and persecution. In Mecca, he confronted harsh opposition from the Quraysh tribe, who fervently sought to suppress the message of monotheism:

> "And those who disbelieve say, 'Do not listen to this Qur'an and speak noisily during [the recitation of] it that perhaps you will overcome.'"

(Fuṣṣilat, 41:26)

The Meccan opposition used everything they could in the attempt to go against monotheism. They employed a great number of strategies, ranging from imposing economic sanctions to inflicting physical persecution upon the followers of Islam in the early stages of Muhammad's SAW prophethood.

4. The Unwavering Resolve of Prophets:

The Prophets AS despite struggling with relentless opposition, exemplify firm resolve and unyielding commitment to their divine mission. It is admirable how they never considered giving up what they believed in. The Qur'an beautifully portrays this extraordinary steadfastness in the face of adversity:

> "So be patient. Indeed, the promise of Allah is truth…"

(ar-Rum, 30:60)

This verse is a strong example of the great strength and resilience required of the prophets and their steadfast followers upon confronting unparalleled opposition.

This thorough examination illuminates the complicated dimensions of the challenges posed by opposition. It sheds light on the profound fortitude and unwavering dedication demonstrated by the prophets of Allah SWT as they navigate the formidable trials while upholding the divine call amidst constant resistance. Through delving into this elaborate exploration, the believers are presented with timeless insights into the resolute nature of the best of all creation, the prophets of Allah SWT and the unconquerable spirit in the face of tough opposition.

> "There has certainly been for you in the Messenger of Allah an excellent pattern1 for anyone whose hope is in Allah and the Last Day…"

(al-Aḥzab, 33:21)

Muslims are encouraged to draw inspiration from the exemplary lives of the prophets as they navigate the trials of their own spiritual journeys. You have all these uplifting examples and teachings, what is stopping you from living in alignment with what you believe to be the truth?

The Divine Support for Prophets:

Despite encountering violent opposition, the prophets of Allah SWT were ensured of unwavering divine support and protection. The Qur'an explicitly conveys this assurance in this verse:

> "Indeed, Allah is with those who fear Him and those who are doers of good."

(an-Naḥl, 16:128)

This sublime divine support serves as the ultimate source of strength for the prophets and their followers in the face of adversities.

Navigating the Struggle: Lessons for Believers

1. **Patience and Perseverance:**

    The Qur'an extols the virtues of patience and perseverance amid relentless opposition. All Muslims are earnestly urged to maintain unshakeable resolve, knowing unequivocally that the ultimate promise of Allah SWT holds true:

    "So be patient. Indeed, the promise of Allah is truth…"

    (ar-Rum, 30:60)

    This verse directs the believers to the indomitable transformative power inherent in patience. Such an attribute is essential to the believers because it is their main strength as they navigate the various challenges posed by persistent opponents.

2. **The Power of Prayer:**

    Islam highlights the profound efficacy of prayer or *salah* in seeking divine guidance and protection. The Qur'an frequently encourages the believers to turn to Allah SWT in sincere supplication, as stated in the narrative of Prophet Yunus (Jonah AS):

    "And [mention] the man of the fish [i.e., Jonah], when he went off in anger and thought that We would not decree [anything] upon him. And he called out within the darknesses, 'There is no deity except You; exalted are You. Indeed, I have been of the wrongdoers.'"

    (al-Anbiya', 21:87)

    This especially emotional narrative draws attention to the importance of prayers and its transformative potential of turning difficult situations into one's favour.

3. Learning from the Past:

The Qur'an repeatedly directs mankind to reflect upon the profound narratives of the past prophets and their opponents. Learning from history is a valuable means to strengthen your faith, as well as gain deep understanding of the recurring patterns of opposition:

"And each [story] We relate to you from the news of the messengers is that by which We make firm your heart…"

(Hud, 11:120)

This verse puts emphasis on the valuable lessons found within the narratives of the prophets' struggles, offering wisdom and strength for the believers.

4. Prophetic Optimism:

The prophets AS, despite confronting unyielding opposition, steadfastly maintained an inherent optimism deeply rooted in their resolute trust in Allah SWT who had sent them. The Qur'an summarises this enduring spirit in the remarkable words of Prophet Musa AS as he stands firmly before Fir'aun (Pharaoh):

"And Moses said, 'My Lord is more knowing [than we or you] of who has come with guidance from Him and to whom will be succession in the home. Indeed, wrongdoers do not succeed.'"

(al-Qaṣaṣ, 28:37)

This remarkable optimism springs from an unshakable faith in the enduring triumph of Allah's divine guidance. It teaches us a lesson of hope and courage whenever we may face adversity in life.

Navigating the Path Amidst Opposition

Learning about the prophets' struggles is a valuable message for all the believers. It inspires them to beautify their characters with the virtues of patience, the resolute power of prayer and the vital educational value from the past. Moreover, it instils the moral spirit of the prophets' optimism and trust in Allah SWT. This is an enduring paradigm for navigating the diverse challenges posed by adversity and their ways of coping in such trying times.

The lives of the prophets of Allah SWT bears witness to a profound and enduring exploration of Allah's divine guidance where we may encounter some resistance from people around us. The prophets of Allah SWT, as the noble bearers of this divine message, were able to confront unyielding challenges posed by their enemies. They have provided living examples on how to behave according to the way of life intended by Allah SWT. We, as Muslim believers, should derive inspiration from these resolute narratives. We must discover the timeless lessons grounded in the foundation of patience, the profound impact of prayer, and the unshakable optimism and trust in Allah's plan for all of us.

Let us contemplate over the previous lessons, let us ponder on the timeless paradigms that persist throughout history. This should help us feel empowered now to navigate any difficult path amidst adversity and face it with firmness, faith and optimism. *Amīn* to that.

A verse to remember, learn by heart and apply if possible:

"So be patient. Indeed, the promise of Allah is truth..."

(ar-Rum, 30:60)

What about your thoughts?

CHAPTER 10
Free Will and Predestination

Free Will: The Gift of Choice

1. The Qur'anic Affirmation of Free Will:

Islam unequivocally affirms the concept of free will, endowing individuals with the capacity to make choices that bear consequences, either rewarding or the opposite direction. You have the opportunity to make free choices, however, you will have to bear responsibility for them. In a hadith *Qudsi*, Allah SWT emphasises this aspect, elucidating the freedom granted to humans:

"...O' My servants, it is but your deeds that I record for you and then recompense you for. So let him who finds good, praise Allah, and let him who finds other than that blame no one but himself."

(Ṣaḥiḥ Muslim 2577a)

In another Qur'anic verse, Allah SWT states:

"And say, 'The truth is from your Lord, so whoever wills—let him believe; and whoever wills—let him disbelieve.'..."

(al-Kahf, 18:29)

In Islam, the affirmation of free will is fundamental to personal empowerment, recognising that every person possesses the capacity for choice and decision-making. The Qur'an, in explaining the essence of this profound gift, highlights the essential nature of individual agency as a fundamental aspect of human existence. Through this divine affirmation, believers are entrusted with the ability to discern between belief and disbelief, right and wrong etc. You are completely free to decide on your own. Moreover, you are also vested with the transformative power to bring change with your conscious decisions and actions. In order for the change to be good, your decisions ought to be virtuous as well.

2. Accountability and Consequences:

The concept of free will in Islam is comprehensively tied to the principle of accountability. The first is followed by the other. Humans are responsible for their choices and actions, and the consequences of those choices unfold in this world as well as the Hereafter. Allah SWT clearly states:

"Whoever does righteousness—it is for his [own] soul; and whoever does evil [does so] against it. And your Lord is not ever unjust to [His] servants."

(Fuṣṣilat, 41:46)

In recognising the importance of accountability, Islam emphasises on the pivotal role of individual responsibility in shaping the course of one's existence. Each choice, whether righteous or marked by transgression, holds inherent consequences—an enduring principle that bears significance in both temporal and spiritual realms. This principle of accountability reminds us of the importance and impact of individual decisions, emphasising the inherent responsibility that comes with our freedom to decide. To put it simply, free will comes with a price. So, you are **FREE** to do what you wish, but you are also **RESPONSIBLE** all actions you take.

3. The Dynamic Nature of Choice:

Islam also teaches us the dynamic nature of our choices, affirming that individuals have the ability to change and shape their destinies by making deliberate decisions and actions through constant *du'a'*. The Prophet Muhammad SAW stated:

"…nothing averts the Divine Decree but supplication…"

(Sunan ibn Majah 90)

It is also stated:

"And those who say, 'Our Lord, avert from us the punishment of Hell. Indeed, its punishment is ever adhering; indeed, it is evil as a settlement and residence.'"

(al-Furqan, 25:65-66)

Within our faith, the dynamic nature of choice reflects a deep truth: individuals have the ability to bring about transformation through conscious decisions, sincere actions and reliance on Allah SWT, who can certainly change their destinies. Our beautiful religion, Islam, in acknowledging the transformative potential of prayer and repentance, emphasises the dynamic interplay between human agency and the enduring capacity for change. This underscores the transformative influence of exercising free will, a testament to the enduring potential for personal growth and spiritual elevation.

4. **Striving for Excellence:**

Free will, in the Islamic framework, becomes a means for individuals to strive for excellence and righteousness. The Qur'an encourages the believers to strive hard in order for them to pursue goodness and moral uprightness. The path towards excellence of the self might be challenging but definitely worthwhile. Not only that, but to compete with one another towards that goodness:

"...So race to [all that is] good. Wherever you may be, Allah will bring you forth [for judgement] all together. Indeed, Allah is over all things competent."

(al-Baqarah, 2:148)

This emphasises the significance of actively pursuing goodness and moral excellence, commanding the believers to continually use their free will only for kindness and moral integrity. The Qur'an acts as a guiding light for humanity, always stressing on the transformative potential that arises from the conscious exercise of free will, motivating individuals to strive, with unwavering commitment and determination, towards the pursuit of good deeds and virtuous actions.

This verse reflects the proactive aspect of free will, urging believers to actively engage in the pursuit of goodness.

Predestination: The Divine Choice

1. Allah's Comprehensive Knowledge:

In parallel with the concept of free will, Allah SWT introduced Himself to us as the only being who possesses the divine attribute of predestination. Allah's knowledge encompasses everything, past, present, and future, forming the foundation of His preordained plan for His creation:

> "Do you not know that Allah knows what is in the heaven and earth? Indeed, that is in a Record. Indeed that, for Allah, is easy."
>
> (al-Ḥajj, 22:70)

This verse emphasises the comprehensive nature of Allah's knowledge, providing the foundation for predestination and what He has intended for His creation before it was created.

2. The Divine Decree:

Predestination in Islam is directly connected to the divine decree. Allah SWT, in His wisdom, has ordained the course of events, and nothing occurs except by His will and permission:

> "Say, 'Never will we be struck except by what Allah has decreed for us; He is our protector.' And upon Allah let the believers rely."
>
> (at-Tawbah, 9:51)

This verse directs us to the fact that we must recognise Allah's decree and rely upon His divine wisdom by accepting those events. Everything that we get is either a blessing or a trial, but we must rest assured because there is a reason for it all.

3. Trusting in Divine Wisdom:

While individuals possess free will in some matters, our faith calls us to trust in the overarching wisdom of Allah's predestination. Indeed, we can find the right balance between using free will in a deliberate way and having complete trust in this predestination. The Qur'an encourages a profound reliance on Allah's divine knowledge and wisdom as indicated in the following verse:

> "And those who disbelieve say, 'Why was the Qur'an not revealed to him all at once?' Thus [it is] that We may strengthen thereby your heart. And We have spaced it distinctly."
>
> (al-Furqan, 25:32)

This verse alludes to the deliberate unfolding of the divine guidance according to Allah's wisdom. The intention of such distinct spacing of the revelation was for better clarity and understanding.

4. The Concept of Qadr:

Qadr, the concept of divine predestination, is a foundational and a core fundamental belief for all the believers. It encompasses everything, including life and death, nourishment, and the unfolding of significant events:

> "Say, 'Never will we be struck except by what Allah has decreed for us; He is our protector.' And upon Allah let the believers rely."
>
> (at-Tawbah, 9:51)

The Harmonious Relationship: Understanding the Paradox

1. The Paradox of Free Will and Predestination:

Islam acknowledges the apparent paradox between free will and predestination. While individuals make choices and are accountable for their actions, the divine plan encompasses everything:

"And We have already created man and know what his soul whispers to him, and We are closer to him than [his] jugular vein."

(Qaf, 50:16)

Let me simplify this for you, hopefully.

Although Allah SWT knows you inside out, because He had fashioned you, He did not impose certain actions of yours. He knew about your actions prior, but He did not intervene or send you angels to help you behave in any sort of manner. He guided you through the Qur'an and the sunnah, but as for the decision, it was up to you.

It is like me knowing about which student in my class is going to fail long before the exams. It has nothing to do with me knowing the future, but through experience, I know who is most likely to pass and who is going to embarrass himself.

Allah SWT knew through His knowledge about our choices. Despite that, he gave us the opportunity to freely act so that we may acknowledge, on the Day of Judgement, that we deserve either rewards or punishment.

2. The Concept of *Tadbīr*:

Allah SWT is described in the Qur'an with the attribute of *Tadbīr* (*Yudabbirul 'Amr*– He arranges the affairs). This attribute reflects Allah's divine orchestration of events in accordance with His preordained and arranged plan for His creation:

"Indeed, your Lord is Allah, who created the heavens and the earth in six days and then established Himself above the Throne, arranging the matter [of His creation]. There is no intercessor except after His permission. That is Allah, your Lord, so worship Him. Then will you not remember?"

(Yunus, 10:3)

"Say, 'Who provides for you from the heaven and the earth? Or who controls hearing and sight and who brings the living out of the dead and brings the dead out of the living and who arranges [every] matter?' They will say, 'Allah', so say, 'Then will you not fear Him?'"

(Yunus, 10:31)

"It is Allah who erected the heavens without pillars that you [can] see; then He established Himself above the Throne and made subject the sun and the moon, each running [its course] for a specified term. He arranges [each] matter; He details the signs that you may, of the meeting with your Lord, be certain."

(ar-Ra'd, 13:2)

"He arranges [each] matter from the heaven to the earth; then it will ascend to Him in a Day, the extent of which is a thousand years of those which you count."

(as-Sajdah, 32:5)

The above verses can be misunderstood to mean that we are like puppets and Allah SWT is arranging everything for us, but this would be an especially limited understanding of Allah's *Qadr*. The broader meaning, as mentioned earlier, is that in numerous aspects of our lives, we do not have choices of our own. For example; where we were born, our skin colour, who our parents are etc. We can neither change these issues, nor have a say in them. However, what I say, what I do and how I react to situations etc., are matters that I CAN control. And so can you.

3. The Role of Supplication and Prayer:

This is what is known as "The weapon of the believer"—*du'a'* or supplication. The transformative power that can alter and change *Qadr*. In fact, it is the ONLY weapon that can negotiate the *Qadr* of Allah SWT. Therefore, the believers are encouraged to turn to Allah SWT in earnest supplications whenever they can.

"The Prophet Muhammad SAW said:

'Nothing extends one's life span but righteousness, nothing averts the Divine Decree but supplication, and nothing deprives a man of provision but the sin that he commits.'"

(Sunan ibn Majah 90)

And the reason is really obvious, because Allah SWT, the most Kind, is closer to us than we might imagine. Thus, He is capable of retracting His plans and replacing them as a result of our sincere *du'a'*. Allah SWT states:

"And when My servants ask you, [O' Muhammad], concerning Me—indeed, I am near. I respond to the invocation of the supplicant when he calls upon Me…"

(al-Baqarah, 2:186)

4. The Wisdom of Allah's Plan:

Ultimately, we as believers, must put our whole trust in the wisdom of Allah's plan for us, even when faced with uncertainties and difficulties. The Qur'an encourages a deep recognition of Allah's divine wisdom:

"And you do not will except that Allah wills. Indeed, Allah is ever Knowing and Wise."

(al-Insan, 76:30)

So put your trust in Him, accept His ultimate judgement, and you will be rewarded abundantly. *Inshā'Allāh.*

Embracing the *Qadr* of Allah SWT

In the journey of faith, understanding the connection between free will and predestination is like appreciating the contrast of various colours. Though they seem at odds with one another, they still form a beautiful piece of art together. The concept of free will acknowledges that we have the power to make choices—decisions that carry consequences. Islam urges us to use this gift responsibly, aligning our actions with the moral guidance revealed in the Qur'an and the life of Prophet Muhammad SAW.

Simultaneously, predestination reminds us that there is a larger plan at play, guided by Allah's ultimate wisdom. It serves as an assurance that even in life's uncertainties, there is a purpose unfolding. The idea of *Qadr* does not negate our choices; it enriches them with deeper meaning and purpose.

This dynamic interconnectedness between the two invites us to embrace the paradox, recognising that our decisions matter, yet there is a divine plan beyond our understanding or control. It is an invitation to humility, acknowledging the vastness of Allah's knowledge compared to our limited minds that may not comprehend everything.

Life is filled with an abundance of challenges, however, as we deal with them, we can find strength in turning to Allah SWT in humility and in *du'a'*. The Qur'an guides us to seek refuge in Allah's mercy and protection, understanding that He is the One controlling all events—a*l-Mudabbir*. It is the sweetest source of comfort, especially when faced with the unknown.

In this lies our submission and surrender to Allah SWT and to His divine harmony. Instead of being confined by fate, we are actually liberated by our trust in Him. We are not alone in facing the challenges of life, He is with us and aware of what we are going through. It is comforting that Allah SWT, the All-Knowing and Wise, is in control, even when our path seems unclear. It is an affirmation that within our choices and Allah's plan, there is room for spiritual growth, resilience, and a deeper connection with Him.

A verse to remember, learn by heart and apply if possible:

"And you do not will except that Allah wills. Indeed, Allah is ever Knowing and Wise."

(al-Insan, 76:30)

What about your thoughts?

CHAPTER 11
Angels and Satan

When it comes to the world of the unseen and the spiritual beings of Allah's creation, angels and the Satan (Iblis) grab the attention. In this chapter, Inshā'Allāh, I intend to explore the essence of angels—created by Allah SWT to purely worship Him, execute His commands, and serve as divine messengers without a free will of their own. Simultaneously, we will also delve into the intriguing character of Satan, a jinn who defied Allah SWT, leading to his fall due to arrogance and disobedience. When we gain a deeper knowledge about the relationship between these spiritual entities, we will be able to understand that angels are agents and servants of Allah SWT and Satan is the tempter, who seeks to lead humanity astray.

Angels: Agents of Divine Obedience

1. **1. Messengers and Worshippers:**

    Angels, in Islam, are part of what we know as the pillars of *iman*. Though we cannot see them, it is incumbent upon us to acknowledge their existence. They are spiritual beings created by Allah SWT from light. Their primary purpose in this existence is to worship Allah SWT tirelessly and obediently fulfil His commands without question. They praise and glorify Allah continuously and without rest:

    "They exalt [Him] night and day [and] do not slacken."

    (al-Anbiya', 21:20)

    Angels are considered to be messengers from Allah SWT who were created to complete tasks assigned by Him with absolute obedience and perfection. Each group of Allah's angels are assigned with a particular job.

2. **Guardians and Recorders:**

Some of these angels are guardians, who are assigned over human beings for the sole purpose of protection and recording their deeds. What a beautiful truth to think of being protected by gentle angels. The two angels on each person's shoulders named Raqib and Atid, record deeds faithfully:

> "For him [i.e., each one] are successive [angels] before and behind him who protect him by the decree of Allah."
>
> (ar-Ra'd, 13:11)

This verse illustrates the meticulous record-keeping entrusted to angels. Not only that, but it is also a reminder for all of us to be vigilant in all that we do, for indeed, we are always being watched.

3. **Jibra'il (Gabriel) - The Archangel:**

Among the prominent angels is Jibra'il, the Archangel, who serves as Allah's chief messenger to all the prophets AS. Jibra'il played a vital role in conveying the revelations of the Qur'an to the Prophet Muhammad SAW:

> "The Trustworthy Spirit [i.e., Gabriel] has brought it down upon your heart…"
>
> (ash-Shu'ara', 26:193-194)

Allah SWT named Jibra'il *al-Amin*, or the trustworthy, to highlight the nature of Allah's creation and the authenticity of the message itself, which was delivered exactly as intended by Allah SWT without any corruption or alteration.

4. **Israfil, Mika'il, 'Izra'il and many others:**

Other notable angels include Israfil, the angel tasked with blowing the trumpet signalling the Day of Judgement; Mika'il, responsible for carrying or pouring rain down from heavens; and the angel of death, was entrusted with the solemn task of taking souls back to Allah SWT:

"Say, 'The angel of death who has been given charge of you will take you…'"

(as-Sajdah, 32:11)

As we mentioned earlier, there is a greater number of angels who were given different tasks and responsibilities. Like Munkar and Nakir—the two angels in charge of questioning people in their graves about their faith and beliefs. Riḍwan and Malik—who watch over Heaven and Hell.

In short, these angels collectively fulfil the plans and commands of Allah SWT.

Satan (*Iblis*): The Defiant Deceiver

1. Origin and Refusal:

Satan, known as *Iblis*, was among the *jinn*—a distinct creation and unseen as well. Satan was created from smokeless fire, unlike angels who were made from light. Though it is a known fact that he was created from fire, he is often remembered by his refusal to bow to Prophet Adam AS. Such arrogance and sense of superiority has led to his expulsion from Allah's favour and *Jannah*:

"And [mention] when We said to the angels, 'Prostrate before Adam'; and they prostrated, except for Iblis. He refused and was arrogant and became of the disbelievers."

(al-Baqarah, 2:34)

This is an essential lesson for all of us to acquire: While Allah SWT does give us multiple opportunities in life, if we disobey Him, it could lead us to nowhere but His wrath.

2. Role as a Tempter:

So, Satan was casted out of *Jannah*, but granted respite until the Day of Judgement. Afterwards, he arrogantly vowed to lead humanity astray. His role is that of a relentless tempter, exploiting human weaknesses to divert them from the righteous path:

> "Indeed, Satan is an enemy to you; so take him as an enemy. He only invites his party to be among the companions of the Blaze."

> (Fāṭir, 35:6)

This verse highlights the essential role of Satan, which is misguidance and deception. Therefore, Allah SWT warns the believers against succumbing to his ways. Stay away from such a roof of evil.

3. Whispers and Distractions:

Satan employs subtle tactics, whispering doubts and desires to humans' hearts and minds. His goal is to create discord and lead believers away from the path of obedience, just like himself. Not only that, but he instils in the hearts and minds of the people, the false idea that he is a sincere advisor, just like how he deceived Adam and Eve AS, he told them, as recorded in the Qur'an:

> "And he swore [by Allah] to them, 'Indeed, I am to you from among the sincere advisors.'"

> (al-A'rāf, 7:21)

Despite the fact that Allah SWT exposes his plans and intentions, many human beings fall prey to these tactics. Be careful not to be one of them because, as the verse shows, *Iblis'* tactics are very subtle and may appeal to our desires and may appear pure and innocent.

4. Seeking Refuge from Satan:

Allah SWT, just as He guides us to the weapon of *du'a'*, He also equips us with other weapons to protect ourselves against Satan's temptations and tricks. One of them is seeking refuge in Allah SWT from Satan's influence. Reciting verses like *ayah al-Kursi* and seeking Allah's protection in daily prayers act as shields against him. Thus, do not let a day pass by without reciting these verses and *du'a's*:

"Say, 'I seek refuge in the Lord of daybreak from the evil of that which He created and from the evil of darkness when it settles.'"

(al-Falaq, 113:1-3)

Lessons for Believers

1. Trusting in Divine Wisdom:

Understanding the roles of angels and satan requires the believers to trust in Allah's divine wisdom and plans, as we have discussed in the previous chapter. The obedient service of angels and the defiant opposition of Satan both play a big part of our understanding. It shows us how to behave in a manner that will not lead us away from the path of Allah SWT:

"And those who have been given knowledge see that what is revealed to you from your Lord is the truth, and it guides to the path of the Exalted in Might, the Praiseworthy."

(Saba', 34:6)

2. Vigilance against Temptation:

Awareness of Satan's tactics calls for vigilance. Therefore, the believers are constantly reminded to resist his temptations and seek refuge in Allah SWT:

"Indeed, Satan is an enemy to you; so take him as an enemy..."

(Fatir, 35:6)

There is no doubt that he is declared as an enemy, he was created by Allah SWT, and Allah is your Creator too. So, if Allah SWT can protect you from his harms, isn't then sensible to keep asking Allah SWT to protect us against his temptations and traps?

3. The Power of Seeking Refuge:

Islam, as a practical religion, comes along with a set of tools to help you seek refuge from satan, the accursed, such as seeking refuge, to guard against satan's influence (to simply say, *'Au'dhubillāhi minash shaytānir rajīm*). The believers are encouraged to adopt these practices into their daily lives, night and day, constantly:

"Say, 'I seek refuge in the Lord of daybreak from the evil of that which He created and from the evil of darkness when it settles.'"

(al-Falaq, 113:1-3)

Navigating the Unseen

As was clearly stated, angels and satan take distinct roles, shaping a dramatic force in which the believers should learn from and become vigilant. A true understanding of each of these roles provides insights into the larger divine plan of Allah SWT and offers lessons for navigating the complexities of the human experience.

Angels stand as a symbol of obedience, reminding us of our role as slaves of Allah SWT. They are messengers of Allah's divine will, guardians appointed by Allah SWT. In the same manner, we are encouraged to convey the message of Islam to everyone around us (messengers), and to protect and take care of one another whenever we can. Our purpose on this earth, aside from worshipping Allah SWT alone, is to share the message of goodness of Islam and live according to it. On the other hand, Satan, in his rebellious pursuit, serves as a reminder of the ongoing struggle against temptations and desires, as well as the importance of seeking refuge and protection in Allah's protective power as the Creator of one and all.

As we navigate this realm, the world of angels and Satan, putting our trust in Allah's wisdom becomes paramount. The roles played by angels and satan are evidently opposing forces and contribute to the unfolding narrative of creation itself. Therefore, the believers are called to be vigilant, resisting the temptations woven into Satan's whispers. At the same time, they are invited to acknowledge the tireless service of angels who are watching over us by Allah's permission.

So long as you struggle and fight hard against Satan's temptations, ultimately, by Allah's will, you can find guidance, protection, and the opportunity to exercise your free will in choosing the path of righteousness.

A verse to remember, learn by heart and apply if possible:

"Indeed, Satan is an enemy to you; so take him as an enemy. He only invites his party to be among the companions of the Blaze."

(Faṭir, 35:6)

What about your thoughts?

CHAPTER 12
Negatives and **Positives:**
Navigating Ethical Dimensions in Islam

As we are about to conclude the book, **Night and Day**, I found myself compelled to discuss the connection between *negative* and *positive* behaviours and actions which could either lead humanity to an awful destination or grant those who obey Allah SWT to live a beautiful life in accordance with Allah's divine principles and values. Negatives include harmful actions, thoughts, or deviations from our ethical standards and whatever else that may displease Allah SWT. In contrast, positives embrace virtues and great qualities that are encouraged by our Creator and His messengers AS.

In this chapter, *Inshā'Allāh*, I will delve into some dimensions of negatives and positives, exploring the ethical landscape through the lens of sincerity, kindness, gratitude and humility. I will also be addressing some of the harmful consequences of addictions to drugs, pornography, and other vices.

Negatives: Straying from Ethical Pathways

1. Harmful Actions and Thoughts:

Negatives, or as they are known in Arabic as haram, encompass a spectrum of harmful actions and thoughts (*though we may not be questioned about our thoughts, unless they lead us to harmful activities*) that are deemed detrimental to individuals and society. These include dishonesty, injustice, backbiting, arrogance, lying, gossiping, cheating and a host of other behaviours contrary to the teachings of Islam:

> "And do not consume one another's wealth unjustly or send it [in bribery] to the rulers in order that [they might aid] you [to] consume a portion of the wealth of the people in sin, while you know [it is unlawful]."

> (al-Baqarah, 2:188)

You see, Islam was not revealed to us for the sole purpose of praying and fasting only. There is certainly more to our beautiful religion. It is a complete way of life. Islam is also the way to establish a just society where everyone feels safe and protected from any harmful force.

2. Addictions and Destructive Behaviours:

Islam addresses the negatives linked with addictive substances and behaviours, recognising their potential to severely harm individuals physically, mentally, and spiritually. This includes the consumption of intoxicants and engaging in harmful and addictive practices such as gambling:

"O' you who have believed, indeed, intoxicants, gambling, [sacrificing on] stone alters [to other than Allah], and divining arrows are but defilement from the work of Satan, so avoid it that you may be successful."

(al-Ma'idah, 5:90)

If an action is deemed as negative, it is automatically classified as harmful, and one should immediately avoid it.

3. Avoidance of Negative Traits:

Islam emphasises the importance of cultivating positive character traits while discouraging the negative ones. Muslims are encouraged to strive against qualities such as pride, envy, and greed, fostering an ethical environment that promotes justice, compassion, and righteousness. In the following verse, you will see how Allah SWT explains the kind of actions He has made forbidden or haram.

"Say, 'Come, I will recite what your Lord has prohibited to you. [He commands] that you not associate anything with Him, and to parents, good treatment, and do not kill your children out of poverty; We will provide for you and them. And do not approach immoralities - what is apparent of them and what is concealed. And do not kill the soul which Allah has forbidden [to be killed] except by [legal] right. This has He instructed you that you may use reason.'"

(al-An'am, 6:151)

The above verse shows that Allah SWT will never classify any action as negative, unless it is harmful to one's self or society at large. Thus, all what is considered negative in Islam is for the sole purpose of your protection. It is comforting to have all these sorted out for us, all we have to do is to obey Allah SWT and His commands.

4. **Repentance and Seeking Forgiveness:**

Recognising human fallibility, Islam provides a pathway for repentance, redemption and seeking forgiveness for the negative actions that we may fall into. The concept of *tawbah* encourages people to return to Allah SWT with sincerity, remorse, and a genuine intention to improve themselves and start afresh:

"Say, 'O' My servants who have transgressed against themselves [by sinning], do not despair of the mercy of Allah. Indeed, Allah forgives all sins. Indeed, it is He who is the Forgiving, the Merciful.'"

(az-Zumar, 39:53)

Therefore, whatever you have done in the past, you still have the chance to shift from the negative to the other bright side. I am certain you would enjoy the light over darkness, anyone would.

Positives: Embracing Virtues in Islam

1. Sincerity and Righteous Intentions:

Positives in Islam, or halal and *mubah* acts, revolve around virtues that guide the believers and all mankind towards righteousness. First and foremost, among them is sincerity (*ikhlas*) in intentions. Whatever you do, should be performed in sincerity. All acts of worship and good deeds are encouraged to be done solely for the pleasure of Allah SWT:

"And they were not commanded except to worship Allah, [being] sincere to Him in religion, inclining to truth, and to establish prayer and to give zakah. And that is the correct religion."

(al-Bayyinah, 98:5)

2. Kindness and Compassion:

Kindness, doing good, known as *ihsan*, and compassion are among the virtues that are highly valued in Islam. All those who believe in Allah SWT and the Last Day are encouraged to treat others with kindness, especially those in need and distress:

"And do not turn your cheek [in contempt] toward people and do not walk through the earth exultantly. Indeed, Allah does not like everyone self-deluded and boastful. And be moderate in your pace and lower your voice; indeed, the most disagreeable of sounds is the voice of donkeys."

(Luqman, 31:18-19)

Upon every verse you look into within the Qur'an, you will find a direction towards that which is good. Either between the relationship to our connection with Allah SWT or towards people. In other words, the Qur'an is the book of goodness. Embrace the teachings wholeheartedly and contribute not only to yourself but also all the people around you.

3. Gratitude and Thankfulness:

Positives also include the attitude of gratitude (*shukr*) for the endless blessings bestowed upon us by Allah SWT. We are encouraged to express gratitude not only through words but also through actions:

"And [remember] when your Lord proclaimed, 'If you are grateful, I will surely increase you [in favour]; but if you deny, indeed, My punishment is severe.'"

(Ibrahim, 14:7)

The Prophet Muhammad SAW deemed showing gratefulness to people simultaneously as a form of showing gratefulness to Allah SWT Himself.

"He who does not thank the people is not thankful to Allah."

(Sunan Abi Dawud 4811)

4. Humility and Modesty:

Humility (*Tawaḍuʿ*) is yet another virtue that underlines the importance of modesty and self-awareness. The believers are encouraged to avoid arrogance and treat others with humility, respect and never to look down upon anyone:

"And the servants of the Most Merciful are those who walk upon the earth easily, and when the ignorant address them [harshly], they say [words of] peace."

(al-Furqan, 25:63)

Why act arrogantly towards anyone if we were all created equal?

Navigating Ethical Dimensions: Lessons for Believers

1. Balancing Negatives and Positives:

Islam calls the believers to find a balance between avoiding harmful actions and embracing positive virtues. The ethical dimensions guide individuals in their interactions with others and their personal development:

"And thus We have made you a median [i.e., just] community that you will be witnesses over the people and the Messenger will be a witness over you…"

(al-Baqarah, 2:143)

Let me clarify the paragraph above.

In no way am I referring to balancing our lives between halal and haram. Halal is obvious and encouraged, and haram is obvious and abhorred. What I mean is that sometimes people would embrace Islam or make several positive changes in their lives while still remaining attached to some of their past negative attitudes or deeds. As a community, we should assist them to gradually embrace the good and filter their lives from negativities. We should certainly share our knowledge of goodness with them and practise patience in doing so. One step at the time.

2. Accountability for Actions:

Muslims are reminded constantly of their accountability for both negatives and positives. Every action, whether negative or positive, carries consequences, and individuals will be held responsible for these deeds:

"So whoever does an atom's weight of good will see it, and whoever does an atom's weight of evil will see it."

(al-Zalzalah, 99:7-8)

So, be watchful of your deeds, and choose wisely.

3. Seeking Help through Prayer:

Islam, as highlighted in previous chapters, is a vastly practical religion. One of the tools that has been provided for us to keep tight ties with Allah SWT is our daily prayers. We were bestowed with regular prayers and supplications so that we may reach out to Allah SWT for assistance, guidance and help:

"Guide us to the straight path-"

(al-Fatiḥah, 1:6)

The above verse, as we all know, IS part of the best of what Allah SWT has revealed. In it, Allah SWT is guiding us on HOW to ask for guidance. For this reason, whenever you can, ask Him to guide you to that which is pleasing to Him.

4. Community Support and Accountability:

Many times, we find ourselves stuck with some sinful activities that are highly powerful and difficult to escape. That is why we are encouraged to foster a supportive community where individuals hold each other accountable for their actions and assist one another when something goes wrong. Positive virtues are reinforced through collective efforts:

"...And cooperate in righteousness and piety, but do not cooperate in sin and aggression..."

(al-Ma'idah, 5:2)

Ethical Excellence in Islam

Negatives/haram and positives/halal and *mubaḥ* in Islam provide a comprehensive ethical framework that guides the believers in their individual and communal lives. Avoiding harmful actions and embodying positive virtues contribute to ethical excellence, fostering a community that upholds justice, compassion, and righteousness.

As we all navigate this temporary *dunya*, remember to hold fast onto the Rope of Allah SWT, the Qur'an, which was revealed as timeless guide, offering clear direction into the ethical dimensions that shape human conduct. And remember again, whether you have chosen the negatives or the positives, Allah SWT is overwatching all that you do. For your own benefit, choose rightly.

A verse to remember, learn by heart and apply if possible:

"...and He is with you wherever you are. And Allah, of what you do, is Seeing."

(al-Ḥadid, 57:4)

What about your thoughts?

FINAL THOUGHTS

Embracing the Diversity of Life's Contrasts

As we are concluding our journey on one of the aspects of Allah's marvellous creation, let us pause for a while and remember the dynamics between opposites that impact the fabric of our very existence. Life is like a colourful piece of art: as much as the bright spots are visible for everyone to see, dark patches are also clearly seen. They both complete the entire image. Colours cannot survive without shades of blacks. Similarly, life will always include moments of kindness and hardship, sadness and happiness, struggle and ease and opposite forces will keep on impacting our lives until the end of our lives.

We dove into some of these dualities that mould our life—the reality of free will and the predetermined fate, the presence of heavenly beings and the nagging voices that drift us away from the right path, and the interaction of good and evil things etc. Highlighting these seemingly contradictory concepts weren't the point; rather, the complexities of life challenges and our spiritual struggles were.

Let us remember the core of this brief research as we wrap up the final part of it. It's not the end, but rather a call to keep moving gracefully amidst life's contradictions and struggles. Our lives are full of forces that are opposite to one another. Your job is to distinguish between that which is beneficial and to resist that which is harmful.

I pray to Allah SWT that you find courage, insight, and comfort as you navigate the challenges and trials of life. Faith in Allah SWT and His guidance, loving others as we love ourselves, and compassion for everyone around us are timeless principles; may they reverberate in our hearts amidst this world of differences and confusions. *Amīn*.

> *"Indeed, this Qur'an guides to that which is most suitable and gives good tidings to the believers who do righteous deeds that they will have a great reward."*
>
> (al-Isra', 17:9)

www.ingramcontent.com/pod-product-compliance
Lightning Source LLC
LaVergne TN
LVHW061617070526
838199LV00078B/7310